GOD'S TOP TEN

By the same author
The Game of Life
It's Always on My Mind

God's Top Ten

J. JOHN

KINGSWAY PUBLICATIONS
EASTBOURNE

First published by Nelson Word Ltd as *Back to God's Basics*
This edition 1997.
Reprinted 1997, 1999.

ISBN 0 85476 666 9

Designed and produced by Bookprint Creative Services
P.O. Box 827, BN21 3JY, England for
KINGSWAY PUBLICATIONS LTD.
Lottbridge Drove, Eastbourne, E. Sussex BN23 6NT.
Printed in Great Britain.

I dedicate this book
to my friend and mentor
Dr Leighton Ford.
A wise guide on the journey.

Contents

Acknowledgements

Many thanks go to my Researcher, Chris Russell—a refreshing tonic, whose insight and perspective were illuminating, challenging and relevant. It was fun working on the book together.

Thank you to my Administrator, Martyn Day, who typed the manuscript and graciously edited and re-edited! He also has a good sense of humour!

I owe a great deal to discussions with various people and especially valued the insights, comments and suggestions from Dr Honor Day regarding Commandment Six: 'Do not murder'. I am also grateful to Dr Norman Shave for updating me on medical practices.

I hosted ten meetings entitled 'Ten Steps to the Good Life' looking at each of the Commandments. I am enormously grateful to the four guest speakers who also contributed to those meetings and stimulated my own thinking—Revd Dr Michael Green, Mrs Rosemary Green, Revd Eric Delve and Revd Peter Lewis. I am also indebted to my Trustees—a source of encouragement and support: Terry and Juanita Baker,

Jamie Colman, Ginny Cooper, Bob Fuller, Rob Richards, Mike Shouler, Ric Thorpe, Richard Turner and Peter Wright.

Last, but not least, grateful thanks to my wife Killy and sons Michael, Simeon and Benjamin. I couldn't understand why Commandment Five: 'Honour your father and mother' was included in the Top Ten; now I have three sons, I'm so pleased it's there!

J. John
Nottingham, England

Preface

The Ten Commandments did not originate with Cecil B. DeMille; although he did use the theme he strayed from the original script!

When we think of all the libraries of law books, it is amazing how wide a span the Ten cover. From the rights of God and the rights of the individual to family rights and property rights. They are the lynchpin for basic morality.

It is obvious that socially, domestically and personally we have problems. We need to get back to basics, but the question is: back to whose basics? If there is a God and he is Creator, should we not at least consult the Maker's instructions?

You shall not covet your neighbour's house. You shall not covet your neighbour's wife, or his manservant or maidservant, his ox or donkey, or anything that belongs to your neighbour.
Exodus 20:17

The grass always seems greener on the other side of the fence. The conversation at the other end of the room always appears more interesting than the conversation you are involved in. However long you take agonising over the menu deciding which dessert to have, when the person's next to you arrives, you realise you have made the wrong choice!

We all know the old adage of keeping up with the Joneses. Is it not often true that we buy things we don't need, with money we don't have, to impress people we don't even like?

As individuals and as a society, materially we have never had it so good. But we've never wanted more so bad. Today we are bombarded with cries of 'more'. Don't be satisfied with what you have. Don't accept second best. Aim high. Think big. The multimillionaire John D. Rockefeller was asked, 'How much money does it take for a person to be really happy?' He replied, 'Just a little bit more.'

Contentment can come to us, we are told. But we'll need to drive a special car, smell especially sensual, and drink the liquid of paradise. Our life, apparently, is made up of the possessions we own, the heights we can reach, the circles we can mix in, the lifestyle we aspire to. The meaning of life is simply of our own making and it can be within our grasp. Can it?

In the UK it has been estimated that the average person spends £1,300 on credit for every £1,000 they earn. We are constantly told, 'Buy now! Pay later!' Nowadays people can be divided into three groups: The Haves, The Have-Nots and the Have-Not-Paid-For-What-They-Haves. The average family ambition is to make as much money as they are spending. But just when we think we're going to make ends meet, someone moves the ends!

If I ask you, who, in your opinion, is *really* living, what's your answer? Are they rich and famous? Do they have money, possessions, opportunities and influential friends? Chances are whatever your answer is, it won't be you. We find it almost impossible to be content with what we are and what we have. We want more. We want bigger and better. We delude ourselves we can't be happy until we've got it. Yet the paradox is—the more we get, the more we want. A glance at history shows us that dictators who grabbed at power didn't rest until they were all-powerful. Even today there are nations grabbing all the land they can, economies laundering as much money as they can, and it's not just true of everyone else, it's true of *us*, you and me.

Is all this just the sorry tale of people living for a dream, a fantasy that can never be achieved? Are most of us therefore designed to die unfulfilled? And those who do achieve 'success', who realise their fulfilment, suddenly when they get there, bemoan not just the trappings that have come with that success, but the loss of something, the fact that they have got to where they aspired to, where they thought true happiness would lie, and in the process discovered it wasn't enough.

On the 8 August 1963 Ronnie Biggs took part in the so-called 'Great Train Robbery' and shared the haul of £2,500,000. Arrested three weeks later, he was jailed for thirty years, but escaped after serving only fifteen months. Since 1970 he has lived in Rio de Janeiro. On the 5 February 1994 *The Guardian* conducted an interview with Biggs and among the questions they asked him was:

Q: When and where were you happiest?
A: Living in Redhill, Surrey, with my wife and children in early 1963.

He confessed he was happiest, not with all that money, but before it had all begun. Salutary reading, isn't it?

OK, Mr Biggs acquired his money illegally. What about someone like tennis superstar Boris Becker, who came close to taking his own life through being overwhelmed by a sense of hopelessness and emptiness? Even though he was enormously successful, something was missing.

I had won Wimbledon twice before, once as the youngest player. I was rich. I had all the material possessions I needed—money, cars, women, everything. I know that this is a cliché, it's the old song from the movie and pop stars who commit suicide. They have everything, and yet they are so unhappy. I had no inner peace.

If money bought happiness, then the wealthiest people would be the happiest—but that's not the case. The suicide rate is not highest among the poorest half of our population, but among the top 25 per cent.

So what should be our attitude to possessions, wealth, achievement? How can we find contentment? The Tenth Commandment points the way.

> You shall not covet your neighbour's house; you shall not covet your neighbour's wife . . . or anything else that belongs to your neighbour.
>
> Exodus 20:17

If there is any word which can be used to describe this society more than any other it is 'covetous'. The dictionary defines covetousness as 'eagerly desiring, grasping another person's property'. We are dealing with thoughts, desires and feelings. Hold on, you say. Are you seriously suggesting that our lack of contentment in this society flows from our wrong desires? Well, yes, I most certainly am!

Although we cannot legislate against coveting, it is the plague of our culture. We are self-centred and so live for our self-fulfilment. That usually means seeing what someone else has got, what someone else is or does and wanting it for ourselves. And have you ever heard anyone apologising for being too covetous?

It is said that each generation gets the advertising it deserves, and that what advertising does is simply to hold a mirror up to society. We cannot blame advertising for greed; it simply reflects and focuses our desires. So we find that the 'caring nineties' are no more caring than previous decades. We cannot scapegoat advertisers for our covetousness, but it does reveal something when the adverts made either side of a TV programme cost more than the programme itself. So insurance companies sell us their insurance by playing on our 'wannabe' culture, and brewers spend around £1.5 million on sixty seconds of film magic. Ancient proverbs have an uncanny truth for this generation:

> What nature requires is obtainable and within easy reach. It is for the superfluous we sweat.
>
> Seneca, Epistles, 1st Century AD

The Bible is just as incisive:

> The lover of money will not be satisfied with money; nor will the lover of wealth with gain.
>
> Ecclesiastes 5:10 NRSV

Why is coveting such a poison?

It brings no happiness or satisfaction

One of the most popular programmes on Radio 4 over the past three decades has been *Desert Island Discs*. Many of us may have a 'fantasy island' and catch ourselves daydreaming about that far off place and what we would take with us to the island. Coveting is about something different. Coveting is a desire to gain, to possess, to have what we really think we could possibly get. We think it's within reach. It's not so much a 'fantasy island'; that's one of the problems. It's about the here and now, and it takes satisfaction away from us. We are always aspiring for something more, which leaves us with discontentment with the way things are for us now.

So what once were luxuries: video, dishwasher, electric shower, CD player, a newer more slick car, we now think are *essential*. It becomes our ambition to get them and our life becomes an obsession with the things we possess or the things that we would like to possess. In contrast Jesus said, 'A person's life does not consist in the abundance of their possessions.'

But it's not just about possessions; it's about the people we are, our personality, the talents we have. We all have our heroes and that's important. But so many of us would like to have the personal qualities that someone else has. We want to have the looks the models have. We want to wear the clothes the fashion leaders wear. We want to be what other people are, or at least have their opportunities and their privileges.

This makes us fundamentally discontented with who we are. There are people with perfect figures, people with high intellects, people with impeccable social skills and because we feel we fall so far short of them we are discontented.

But if we think this is just a problem in the commercial we are mistaken. Within politics there is a constant craving, a coveting for the prestige that others have. The aim is to get as high as you can. There is a coveting of power, influence and fame. Sadly even the church is riddled with covetousness.

It's no wonder the advertising campaign for 'Hush

Puppies' is so effective when it coins the slogan, 'Be comfortable with who you are.' For that's what we all want. But we all covet what others have. So we are never satisfied.

It brings no permanence

The dissatisfaction that comes with coveting brings with it a real lack of permanence. Our coveting never stands still. It always grows and wants something bigger and slicker and more impressive. We are always thirsting for more. In 1851, Schopenhaur said coveting '. . . is like sea water; the more we drink, the thirstier we become'.

Things satisfy us for a while, then they lose their thrill. Can you remember everything you got last Christmas? If we put our ear to the wardrobe we can hear the moths eating the designer labels. The more we covet, the more we want to acquire. We find ourselves in the quicksand of our own making, restless, with everything suddenly seeming temporary and so disposable. Someone said that one of the characteristics of today's culture is that we enjoy purchasing new things more than we ever enjoy using them or wearing them. The thrill is in the buying. Once we've acquired it, we simply move on and try to take hold of more, or something different.

The philosopher Nietzsche said, 'We grow weary of those things which we most desire.'

Coveting brings no permanence.

What we covet never delivers what we think it promises.

Money can buy medicine, but it cannot buy health.
Money can buy a house, but not a home.
Money can buy companionship, but not friendship.
Money can buy entertainment, but not happiness.
Money can buy food, but not appetite.
Money can buy a bed, but not sleep.

We have our hands full of the things we wanted, but our hearts are still empty. The desert is still inside. T. S. Eliot poetically summed it up in these words:

> The desert is not only remote in southern tropics,
> The desert is not only around the corner,
> The desert is squeezed in the tube train next to you,
> The desert is in the heart of your brother
>
> Choruses from The Rock I

It breeds envy and violence

There have been many discussions recently about the effect of the media and publicity images on the way people behave, particularly those who commit crimes. I am aware that this area is very complex, and I certainly don't claim to be an expert but isn't it obvious that the images we are consciously or even unconsciously taking in have an effect on our behaviour? Try booking a public tennis court just after Wimbledon fortnight and you will find most of the country has been inspired by watching the professionals to get out on the court themselves. Of course, what we see, the possessions we are supposed to obtain, the images we are fed have an effect on us. And coveting has an effect on how we treat people.

If we covet something somebody else has, we envy them. We find many reasons inside our head to explain why such and such a person does not deserve something or a certain kind of lifestyle and why we are worthy of it. We can become bitter and hostile towards those who have what we want, or are people we would like to be. So covetousness can affect our relationships.

Covetousness affects our society by spreading envy and violence. Men and women who so desire what someone else has, or what someone else can do for them commit grievous and hideous acts of violence and destruction on their fellow human beings and society's institutions.

Where does so much crime begin? In the act of coveting, in the desires and scheming inside the mind to have what someone else has.

In the Bible Jesus' brother said something very wise on this issue:

> Those conflicts and disputes among you, where do they come from? Do they not come from your cravings at war within you? You want something and do not have it; so you commit murder. And you covet something and cannot have it; so you engage in disputes and conflicts.
>
> James 4:1–2 NRSV

Coveting leads to envy when we can't or don't get what we want, and causes a significant section of our population to perpetrate acts of violence and crime against each other.

But it's not just true of individuals. The history of

the world has seen one country covet another country's land, invariably leading to invasion and war.

Millions upon millions of men and women have died fighting to realise their country's covetous desires, and even more have died defending their countries from covetous neighbours.

Covetousness also breeds exploitation and unrest within countries. Now I'm not saying that people who are oppressed and downtrodden should not work for liberation. The election of Nelson Mandela as President of South Africa was a momentous landmark in the country's history. To obtain freedom from apartheid and bury the evil that exploited the black and so-called 'coloured' majorities is one thing—but where did that evil begin? It began when Europeans went to one of the most beautiful countries in the world, coveting it for themselves and taking possession of it from the indigenous people and using those people to serve their covetous evil ends. The covetousness which God forbids does not exclude those who are downtrodden from wanting, dreaming and working for freedom.

But some covetousness, especially for more money, does cause social unrest. Some strikes seem to be simply about an inherent greed with people desiring more and more. Society sees the injustice of covetous directors of companies who award themselves huge salary increases, while everyone else tightens their belts because of a recession. But the storm of protest has more than just a tinge of envy in it. It's not that it is objectively wrong; it's that it's not fair on me. I'm envious of someone having all that extra money, while I have to do with less.

In the nineteenth century Cardinal de Retz summed up our condition in the following words: 'The greatest of all secrets is knowing how to reduce the force of envy.'

So if 'desire is the very essence of man' (Spinoza, *Ethics*, 1677), how can we live lives of contentment, not serving as prisoners under our covetousness?

Be realistic

One of the first things we must do is have a realistic view of ourselves and, just as importantly, of other people. If we do this we will soon learn that we have an idealised picture of other people's lives; their circumstances and their relationships aren't at all as glamorous as they appear and as we might have first thought.

Let's not fall for the lies which the world tries and usually succeeds to sell us, that 'if only . . .' we had this or that we would live lives of blissful happiness and contentment. Don't confuse making a living with making a life. Realise that there is a whole lot more going on than just the here and now.

Things do not give us permanent happiness, and things cannot give us permanent security. If we are going to have security it must be in something that will not be taken away. We can lose our wealth and our jobs overnight. In October 1987 in London millions of pounds were wiped off the Stock Exchange. Many became bankrupt. Security into insecurity in minutes.

Alexander the Great inherited one empire and conquered another. He literally had the East and the West by the age of thirty-three. He quickly became disillusioned with life because of all that he had, much like King Solomon, understanding that possessions could not bring happiness. He had enough presence of mind to request that when he died he would have his hands open, so that people who came to view his body would realise that the man who owned the whole world had left it with nothing.

Focus on relationships not things

Although, as we have said, we can obviously be covetous over relationships, if we actually focus on the person in their own right, and not on what they have, either in terms of possessions or talents, or what they can do for us, then we can invest our time and energy in people. So we take our eyes from our desires to the other person and love them, not attempting to use them to fulfil our own covetous desires.

Give generously

Nothing can give more happiness than being able to alleviate people's needs and suffering. We do have a topsy-turvy world when we value and honour those who hoard wealth and possessions and despise those who give until they have barely enough for themselves (e.g. Mother Teresa). But there is a deep-down nagging respect and admiration for them because they seem somehow to have lifted themselves above this covetous generation.

Now obviously I'm not saying we must not have

anything of our own. But if it is possible, we will find that giving to those with greater needs (in comparison to our own wants) is a great antidote to coveting.

Evaluate priorities regularly

Complacency is very dangerous. Because materialism has a subtle influence, Jesus Christ warned us to be on our guard:

> Take care! Be on your guard against all kinds of greed.
> Luke 12:15 NRSV

Coveting can sneak up on us. We need to check ourselves:

- What do we think of the most?
- What do we talk of the most?
- What do we invest our time and energy in the most?

If all this talk of coveting, happiness, priorities and satisfaction has left you wondering what life is all about; if your life is often characterised by discontentment, you are realising that there is something fundamentally more to life.

God's basics have got us one step down the ladder to what really matters. We need to learn the lesson that coveting does not bring contentment. Or as one philosopher, Mick Jagger, put it, 'I can't get no satisfaction'!

The command God gave three and a half thousand years ago is hugely relevant for us today. Our society, our world, our own lives would be so transformed if we didn't covet.

The grass is not greener over that side of the fence. The grass is not greener over this side of the fence. The grass is greener when you water it!

> *You shall not give false testimony against your neighbour.*
> Exodus 20:16

Someone wrote in to a national newspaper asking the question, 'If I say, "I always tell lies," am I telling the truth?' Among the answers given was the following:

> The human race is made up of three types of person: saints who always tell the truth, devils who always tell lies and sinners who sometimes tell the truth and sometimes tell lies. Logically a saint cannot say, 'I always tell lies' since this would be a lie. A devil cannot say 'I always tell lies' since this would be the truth. Only a sinner can logically say, 'I always tell lies,' and this would be a lie.

We would all, I would hazard to guess, place ourselves in the last category!

Our tongue takes up less than 0.045 per cent of our body weight, but it is the greatest asset we have and the most potentially destructive possession we own.

Aesop, the philosopher of the Fables, was asked one day what was the most powerful thing in the world. 'The tongue,' he replied. And what is the most harmful thing in the world? 'The tongue,' he replied once more.

The Ninth Commandment, 'You shall not bear false witness', raises the question of truth and the power of words. It confronts many of the issues which have been on the front pages of our newspapers. As a nation we go up-in-arms at any idea that we have been lied to by our politicians, by the police or by other countries. Most of us agree that telling a lie is a bad thing. Treason and perjury are still regarded as two of the most serious crimes in many countries. In the House of Commons it is against Parliamentary rules to mislead the House or to call anyone a 'liar'. Yet this is the generation in which we have been introduced by our national leaders to phrases such as being 'economical with the truth'.

It's easy to think this Commandment just refers to others . . . When was the last time you used any of these phrases?

- Give me your number and I'll call you back.
- The cheque is in the post.
- This won't take a minute.
- Let's have lunch sometime.
- I'll start my diet tomorrow.
- How nice to see you again.
- I'm sorry he's not available at the moment . . .

Dr Leonard Keiller invented the lie detector, and surveyed more than 25,000 people in devising the instrument. After testing all those people he concluded that people are basically dishonest. Questions of truth and lying pervade all that is said or left unsaid in our families, our working relationships, our communities and the media.

This Commandment affects false witness in court, gossip over coffee in the kitchen, misrepresentation in a business deal, insinuation in a speech, equivocation in the written word, massaging the figures in the end of year report, holding back the truth from the investigating authorities, slander in the newspaper. The way we use words is important and that's an understatement.

When did we first tell a lie? If you are anything like me, it was while you were in nappies! By the time some children are ten they are able to look at their parents or teachers in the eye and lie to them and feel no sense of guilt. And we all know the old catchphrase, 'Sticks and stones may break my bones but words will never hurt me', but we have all been more deeply wounded by words than by any physical assault. Has there ever been a greater untruth sung in the playgrounds?

Lies affect the liar. They affect our relationships with those we lie to. We find ourselves having to lie more to cover up the previous lies and soon we learn to trust no one and begin to doubt ourselves. We get to the point where we become such compulsive liars that we cannot help lying and begin to believe the lies we tell unconsciously to others, and the line between truth and lies, fact and fantasy becomes, not just blurred, but extinct. Bette Midler, the larger than life American actress confessed, 'I never know how much of what I say is true.'

Our words are also irretrievable; once said we cannot take them back. Many of us will have been on the giving and receiving end of this and know the awful truth. There is a story of a man who went to see a monk during the medieval ages. He told the monk that he had sinned because he had been gossiping and spreading rumours about someone in the local town. What should he do? The monk told him to go and put a feather on every doorstep in the town. The man rushed away and fulfilled his penance as quickly as possible and returned to the monk. The monk then told him to go and pick up the feathers. The man told the monk that that was impossible as they would have been blown by the wind and would be miles away. Quietly the monk told the man that was exactly what was happening with his careless and maliciously spoken words.

Human beings have a unique ability to communicate. We speak words and make them rhyme and call them poetry; set them to music and record them and sell them to millions; publish them, read them, make up games with them, make jokes out of them. Our ability to communicate in such a sophisticated manner sets us apart from the non-human creation. But there is something slightly ironic about a generation which is fascinated by the way in which dolphins communicate, yet are such masters at misleading each other in communication!

We all know that what we say is important, but why is lying so wrong? Is it just that we might get found out or is there something more fundamentally wrong with it?

God in the dock

God is true. In him there is no falsehood. The Bible contrasts God with his opposites. Throughout the Bible we see contrasts between light and darkness; good and evil; truth and lies; right and wrong; and between love and hatred. God does not just possess the qualities of light, good, truth and love. He *is* light: 'In him there is no darkness at all' (1 John 1:5). He is good; he is true and cannot lie. 'God is not man, that he should lie . . . has he said, and will he not do it? Or has he spoken and will he not fulfil it?' (Numbers 23:19 RSV). God is incapable of lying. He never lies (Titus 1:2). Contrasted to God is the devil who is described as the 'father of lies', a title he earns from his first encounter with human beings.

God does not lie, mislead, distort, or hurt by malicious words, so the standard is laid out for us. It is wrong to bear false testimony because God is truth, because he cannot bear false testimony and as we are made in his image we are made to live truthful lives. Every time we lie we distort his image in us and move further away from his plans for us and his plans for our friendships, communities and nations.

Society erodes without truth

In his chilling novel *Nineteen Eighty-Four* George Orwell tells how the dictatorial one-party state has a building for the state department, 'The Ministry of Truth'. On the side of the building are three slogans:

War is peace.
Freedom is slavery.
Ignorance is strength.

In any democratic society we value truth above all else. Justice depends on it. Business dealing depends on it. Our diplomats depend on it in foreign relations. Truth is a vital element of our society. However, as St Augustine remarked, 'When regard for truth has been broken down or even slightly weakened, all things will remain doubtful.'

The past few years have seen many reversals of 'miscarriages of justice' by the Court of Appeal—the highest appeal court in the land. None of these is more graphically portrayed than in the film *In the Name of the Father* which told the story of the Guildford Four, who were jailed in 1979 for the IRA bombing of a pub in Guildford. It was nearly a decade and a half later that it came to light that the evidence against the men was not substantial enough to have brought a conviction, and that questionable means had been employed to get the verdict desired by the crime squad involved. The truth had not been told in court and the repercussions had not only sent four innocent men to prison, but had brought the whole legal and criminal investigative procedure into serious doubt.

In no other age has the adage, 'There are lies, damned lies and statistics' been more true. Some will do anything to prove their point of view from statistics. The former Archbishop of York, Stuart Blanch, wrote, 'We are living in a world where the lie is not just a hasty response to an unwelcome situation, but an instrument of policy.'

The Watergate scandal in the USA is a famous example of how a government lost its credibility because of the lies that had been told and sanctioned at the very highest level. In May 1994 the man who fell furthest in that scandal, the President, Richard Nixon, died. In all the remembrance and assessment of his life, one thing could not be forgotten; he was the man who had lied to Congress. His country never forgot and never trusted him again. It hung like a millstone around his neck and remained the recurring memory of the man's whole life and work.

But we delude ourselves if we think it's only the leaders of countries who lie. We may throw our arms up in despair at the lack of integrity in those in leadership, but what about us?

Which papers sell the most in this country? Which TV programmes have the highest audience figures? Which magazines have the highest circulation? Are not the most popular things the scandalous, the gossip-mongering journals, the suggestive programmes, the magazines which dish the dirt? We are all people who 'delight in lies' as the Bible says (Psalm 62:4). We prick our ears up at gossip, we swallow all the scandalous talk we can about others, the more juicy it is the better.

Advertising has become so lucrative that companies spend millions on selling their product. We are continually sold the lie that we need their wares, we cannot do without them, that they are essential to our daily living or if we want a successful social life. We have probably had over two dozen 'new improvements' on every washing powder. Advertisers can easily fall into peddling lies. So we have an advertising standards council who review all adverts for truth, and if they are deemed to be misleading they are withdrawn and the company fined. The Press Complaints Commission was set up to deal with the same problems in the press. And barely a month goes by without some libel case between a newspaper and a person claiming that what was written about them was untrue, and the awards for such cases can run into hundreds of thousands of pounds. But still newspapers rely on scandal and nudity to boost their sales and sales pitches guarantee their wares with exaggeration. Who can we afford to trust? Issues of truth and honesty, false witness and dishonesty are all about us.

Dishonesty undermines our personal relationships

When we recognise the need for honesty in affairs of state, and in the media, we become aware that the spotlight turns onto us. Honesty is the key element of our relationships with each other as human beings. When we are cheated, when we are let down, when we know that rumours have been spread about us behind our back, we feel hurt and wounded. And once a so-called close friend has let us down badly by being untruthful once, we find it almost impossible to rebuild the level of trust to what it previously was. Dishonesty wrecks friendships.

And what about gossip?

Earl Wilson once said, 'Gossip is when you hear something you like about someone you don't.' Basically gossip is repeating private information to someone who is part of neither the problem nor the solution. The book of Proverbs talks a lot about gossip:

> Without wood a fire goes out, without gossip a quarrel dies down. The words of a gossip are like choice morsels, they go down to a man's inmost parts.
>
> Proverbs 26:20,22

We would be a whole lot healthier if we confessed our own errors and faults rather than what we thought someone else's were.

Gossip also ruins friendships. Have you ever walked into a room and been met by a stony silence, and you knew that they had all just been talking about you? How does that make you feel? It completely destroys any feeling of trust, it drives us into ourselves. And what about the biggest gossip you know? Do you trust them with your deepest secrets? No, of course you don't, for we know that the one who brings gossip also carries it. Someone once said, 'The person who will gossip to you will gossip about you.' Dishonesty wrecks friendships.

It also wrecks personality. Some people become so good at spinning yarns, at telling what they think are little 'white lies' which on the whole always portray them in the best light possible, that in their own mind the line between what is true and what is false becomes blurred and they begin to believe the lies about themselves. They begin to live the lie, constantly having to put on an attractive persona for the outside world.

It is very telling that Jesus Christ used the term 'hypocrite' which literally means 'play-actor' over twenty times. Each time it is directed against people who spoke one thing but lived another. Jesus called them white-washed graves—who looked all clean on the outside, but inside they were like death warmed up. God can see through the veneer which fools everyone else, which even fools ourselves sometimes. God knows us better than we know ourselves.

Truth is necessary for our national life, our judicial system, our political system, our communities, our media and for our personal relationships and our own self-understanding. Yet we have slipped away as a society and as individuals from any standards of genuine honesty. How untrusting we are as a society and as individuals.

Our hearts are in a mess

The Old Testament prophet Jeremiah said, 'The heart is deceitful above all things . . . who can understand it?' (Jeremiah 17:9). Our hearts are deceitful and because we have deceitful hearts we speak and live deceitfully.

Jesus said, 'How can you speak good things when you are evil? For out of the abundance of the heart the mouth speaks' (Matthew 12:34 RSV).

So what is in our hearts that causes us to be dishonest?

Fear

We are afraid of what might happen if we tell the truth. Sometimes we lie when we do not have the courage to say no. How many times have we said, 'I can't' when we really meant 'I don't want to'?

Pride

When we put ourselves in a better light, we lie. We want to impress people. We all know that CVs and job application forms are the height of creative writing! We cannot cope with not looking better than we really know ourselves to be, so we lie.

Selfishness

We are dishonest if we can profit by it. It is in our benefit. Why do you think second-hand car salesmen have got the reputation they have?

The beginning of honesty is the confession of dishonesty. We lie because we gain by it. We are habitual and automatic liars when our own comfort is at stake, unblushingly telling untruths for self-advantage until lying becomes a way of life.

So, what can we do about it?

Let us refuse to give or receive gossip

> A gossip betrays a confidence, but a trustworthy man keeps a secret.
>
> Proverbs 11:13

When we are tempted to pass on a rumour, we ought to stop and ask ourselves, 'Am I willing to sponsor this story by signing my name to it?' That's a key, because if we are not willing to put our name to it, we shouldn't share it, because when we do share it, we are sponsoring it.

'Well, I was just speaking off the record.'

Nothing is ever off the record. If we say it then we are going to be quoted. If we don't want to be quoted then we mustn't say it.

The Ninth Commandment says, 'Tell the truth.' But it is not a licence to blow people away with the truth. Just because something is true does not give us the right to shout it.

Not only should we not gossip, but we need also to

refuse to listen to it. We mustn't just sit and let someone go on and on, while we suck it up like a vacuum cleaner. We need to challenge the speaker. Have you checked that out with the source? It's amazing how many people back off when asked for verification of a rumour.

I throw anonymous letters in the dustbin. Someone might say, 'There's been some talk.' Who said it? Because it is impossible to evaluate a statement if we don't know where it came from.

The context makes a big difference.

The Bible's antidote is typically practical.

Everyone should be quick to listen, slow to speak and slow to become angry.

James 1:19

A healthy motto is: 'Make sure your brain is engaged before putting your mouth into gear.'

It expresses a Jesus-like approach to life, too. The more Jesus was provoked, the less he actually said.

Towards the end of his life, Jesus became a victim of those who broke the Ninth Commandment literally. In the court of the Sanhedrin, 'many testified falsely against him'. The High Priest stood up before them and asked Jesus, 'Are you not going to answer?' But Jesus remained silent and gave no reply.

And yet in the midst of these topsy-turvy happenings, in which the truth is being condemned to death because of lies, the Roman Governor, Pontius Pilate, asked one of the most profound questions men and women have ever asked: 'What is truth?' The irony is that the truth was standing right in front of his eyes but because he had been completely blinded by lies, he could not see.

Let us keep our promises

> He who keeps his oath even when it hurts . . . will never be shaken.
>
> Psalm 15:4–5

The mark of integrity is that promises are kept.

Jesus told his followers that their 'yes' should mean yes and their 'no' should mean no. Let us endeavour to be true to our word. It will mean we have to think before we commit ourselves to things. It will cut out casual promises.

> Like clouds and wind without rain is a man who boasts of gifts he does not give.
>
> Proverbs 25:14

We have all been very hurt by people who've broken their promises to us and we've probably let down many people in the same way. There are a lot of great talkers in the world. But a person who will be respected keeps a promise.

Let us make it our goal to be encouragers

The Bible says: 'Do not let any unwholesome talk come out of your mouth, but only what is helpful for building others up according to their needs, that it may benefit those who listen' (Ephesians 4:29).

One minister I knew, the late Alan Redpath, in one of his churches, was going through a tough time. At one meeting he said, 'We are going to start an MEF. Who wants to join MEF, Mutual Encouragement Fellowship? We are going to encourage each other rather than discourage each other. How many of you want to join?' Everyone raised their hands. He said, 'There is only one qualification you need to join this: "I will think before I speak".'

He came up with this acrostic: THINK. Five questions to ask yourself before you say something:

T — is it true?
H — will it help?
I — is it inspiring?
N — is it necessary?
K — is it kind?

A key to healthy living—honesty

With honesty we can live life with a clear conscience.

> No man has a good enough memory to be a successful liar.
>
> Abraham Lincoln

> If you always tell the truth, you never have to remember anything.
>
> Mark Twain

We live in an age of truth-decay. Honesty is not respected. Let us mean what we say and say what we mean.

It costs to be honest. It's often easier to lie. It costs—but it also pays.

The benefit is a clear conscience. The benefit is peace of mind. The benefit of an honest society for us all would be huge. Let us therefore desire personal and corporate integrity and honesty.

You shall not steal.
Exodus 20:15

Stealing horrifies most of us, especially when it affects us personally. I suppose many of us have experienced at first hand the misery of returning home to find that we have had intruders who have taken property that was ours. I certainly have. Not only do we feel that our private space has been violated, but it makes us feel vulnerable and fearful. Someone has been through our personal things and knows something of our private life and have taken from us things that were precious. We may not necessarily be wounded by the financial loss, but we certainly are when items are taken which were special to us because of their sentimental value. And we demand justice. We want to see the culprit taken to court and punished.

On the other hand, consider the following situations. We may have to go to a business meeting using public transport. We are able to save money using a rail card or other offer, but as the business is paying we claim for the full amount. Or we may be horrified by how much it costs to post our Christmas cards and so we slip them through the company's franking system. Or we take our address book into work and make a few of those personal calls from the office when things are quiet; it will save our phone bill. After all, everyone does it . . .

An income tax analysis reported the following: 'Precise statistics are impossible to obtain, since no one knows the amount of income that escapes taxation through evasion, unrecorded financial transactions and other similar activities. Inland Revenue officials estimate that the amount is between five and eleven billion pounds a year.'

Government economic policy has to take into account that some of the highest earners in this country will not pay tax, keeping their money in offshore bank accounts and the like. And at the other end of the scale are those who fiddle Social Security benefits.

We don't like to call this stealing, so we talk about borrowing, using, shrewdness or playing the system. Society has this inconsistent view of stealing. On the one hand we maintain that one should not steal. There is a universal condemnation of those who break in to the homes of the elderly for a few pounds, of armed robbers, or business tycoons who steal from the company pension scheme, or armies which march into another country and take it over. We still give life sentences for armed robbery, because we think stealing is wrong.

On the other hand, if you cast your mind back to the film *Buster*, which told of Ronnie Biggs and his gang and the Great Train Robbery, did we cast a romantic light on crime by the making of such a film? Do we begin to be intrigued by crime, to admire those who are successful at it and cease to worry about the principles involved? Biggs himself, still in exile in Rio de Janeiro, Brazil, said once that he thought 'the majority of clear-thinking people in England would be in favour of me being pardoned'.

Those who commit such crimes are not without standards; they just believe that they can justify their actions. Do I think like that? Am I consistent? Or do I justify to myself the things that I know are wrong?

Who do things belong to?

'The world and all that is in it is mine,' says the Lord.
Psalm 50:12

A Jewish commentary has subtitled this Commandment 'The Sanctity of Property'. We are not to take what belongs to someone else. When the Commandment was first given, property meant livelihood. In those days, if you stole someone's cattle, you left them in dire straits. There were no insurance policies then!

But the most important principle behind the Commandment is that property first and foremost belongs to God. God has only given us stewardship of the things we own. Our possessions are on loan from him.

There is a story in the Bible about a vineyard. King Ahab and Queen Jezebel decided they liked the look of it, but it belonged to a man named Naboth, who did not take kindly to the king's suggestion that he sell his family land. So the pair decided to kill Naboth and take possession of the vineyard. God's judgement on them was strong and unequivocal. God's representative told the king and queen that their days were numbered and they were to die in a gruesome and horrible way. Why? Because the land had been given to Naboth's forebears as a gift from God. Ahab and Jezebel had no right to take it. God is not indifferent when his laws are broken.

The Bible recognises the rights of personal property, but it does not condone the grabbing of wealth at the expense of others. Justice and mercy are the principles that permeate the Bible, and God is a merciful God who hates injustice. He will not vindicate anyone who amasses wealth unjustly. We will be held accountable for what we do with what God gives us.

Theft is therefore taking from God what he has given to another person. It destroys God's plans. It is a challenge to God's authority. And as with every other occasion when we go against what God has commanded, we have to pay the price. Because like all disobedience, it affects not only our relationship with him, but also sows the seeds for destruction in the world we live in.

A world without stealing

Just imagine what our world would be like if there were no stealing. Think how it would affect our relationships and our society if we could trust one another— no burglar alarms or complex security systems; everyone would be able to sleep at night, free of the fear of burglars.

Just think how society has had to change to accommodate the reality of stealing. In our homes, shops, offices, banks—even in hospitals. In the Queen's Medical Centre in Nottingham, near where I live, and where my three sons were born, baby Abbie Humphries was stolen. There was a happy ending when Abbie was found and rescued, but what pain and anguish that act of theft caused.

A friend of mine who worked at a major London department store one summer told me that the internal security for staff was so tight that every day their bags were searched for stolen property. Millions of pounds have to be written off each year because of theft. It ruins businesses when employees are involved in dishonest practices. It affects industrial relations when people fiddle the system.

Why do we do it?

As we saw in Chapter One covetousness, or greed, is what makes us take what belongs to others. We imagine it will enable us to have a better quality of life. We have bought the lie that life is made up of what we own: wealth, possessions, the here-and-now. We have a distorted sense of priorities.

Stealing also comes from a lack of responsibility, a refusal to see ourselves as part of a wider picture. We don't want to accept the level of personal accountability that we should. We try to get away with paying as little tax as possible, whereas Jesus taught that we should pay to 'Caesar what belongs to Caesar and to God what belongs to God'. He gave no licence to people to shirk the paying of taxes. Jesus was not contemptuous of wealth, as some socialists are, but nor did he condone undue profits.

We need to understand that our anxiety for gain often goes against the laws of God. Those who prosper materially often do so at the expense of their conscience, and those who cheat live with the fear of being found out. To forsake a good conscience and peace of mind for the sake of more prosperity seems a bad choice. One man I heard about had been working all his life in a factory. When it was discovered that he had 'taken' some odd bits and pieces from the factory his family was devastated, his work colleagues were surprised, and he was completely destroyed. He never recovered from the shame, and died within a year.

What can we do?

It is vital that we take a good look at ourselves to see where we are being dishonest, where we have taken from others in our family, our employers, the state. There may be many areas where we have to put things right, and we may stand out as different or odd.

One person who used to work at the Ministry of Defence felt very strongly that he ought to take a firm line on stealing. Like many other organisations, the MOD employs people with some very different views on the matter. For example, one man's house was completely furnished with equipment from a battleship. But this person was not like that. He did make the most of the free photocopying and the personal phone and the expenses claim, but he gently began to cut all that out. At first it was strange to walk past all his colleagues and go outside the office to a payphone to make his private calls. He would walk quite a long way during his lunch break to get some photocopying done. His actions were noted, and at first there was some muted mocking, but gradually the department began to work in a similar vein. Eventually that department became the most efficient and the most motivated.

We have to start with ourselves. We have to restore what is not ours to the rightful owner. When I reached the realisation that I had things which weren't mine I decided the only thing to do was to return them. So I gathered up about eighteen books, including some encyclopedias, that I had stolen from a large bookshop in London and took them back. The first sales assistant nearly fainted and I had to explain to the manager that I had stolen the books but had now become a Christian and would be quite happy to start paying for them. He was so stunned by my testimony that he said I did not need to pay him anything. Wouldn't it be good to have a national Return-What-We've-'Borrowed' Day!

Can you see how much difference this change in behaviour would make to your life, your friendships, your family, your hobbies? It will be hard; if you send in an expense claim consistently lower than your colleagues' you may ruffle a few feathers, because it may challenge what has long been an accepted way of life. But do not be deceived; it is the right way forward in the long run.

Also, as well as dealing with ourselves we must look further afield. We must be those who champion what is right and do not support institutionalised stealing.

This refers to so many things: big business, politics and policies, levels of taxation and foreign policy.

Another area is the way we steal from the environment, the way we take from the resources of the earth and so jeopardise the future for generations to come. We have used and abused the resources of the world to the extent that if we don't change the way we treat the world, it may be irrevocably damaged. The statistics are horrifying, they tell of the destruction of the rain forests, holes in the ozone layer, global warming, etc. We must do all we can to ensure that the Government acts responsibly and takes seriously its role as legislator in protecting the environment. But we can start with ourselves. We can treat the world with respect, not stealing from it. Perhaps we could start by recycling: paper, aluminium cans, glass—there are recycling centres springing up all across the country. We can drive cars which use unleaded petrol. We have not been set on this earth to use and abuse it at our will. We are not the gods of this earth, but rather we are stewards who have a responsibility to treat that which God has entrusted to us with respect and dignity.

One more issue which I want to mention before we move off this chapter. It is common knowledge that here in the West, where less than one third of the world's population live, we use over two thirds of the world's resources. And that includes the food we eat, the clothes we wear, and the causes we support. This is a huge issue, and I for one have realised that for too long we have been stealing that which is not ours from other nations. There are a number of things I can do to change. I can refuse to support those companies that are known to be exploiting less well-off parts of the world. I can buy coffee and tea which is from a company which guarantees that those who worked in the production of it are not being stolen from in regards to their labour and lifestyle. Companies such as Café Direct offer help to those who have so long been exploited by foreign countries such as ours simply for our own convenience. But also I can give. In comparison to so much of the world we are so wealthy in the West, sometimes to a staggering extent. For instance a Hollywood dog earns the same in one day as some workers in developing countries earn in a year.

Now we might not think our salary or income to be that high, but we still have plenty compared to so many others. And I would encourage you to give some of it away. Perhaps you could support a group you are involved with: a local children's hospital, a hospice, a local community project. And also be ready to support the one-off causes, the appeals for money for supplying aid to those most in need. We cannot give to everyone, but we can give to some. My children, Michael (10) and Simeon (7) and Benjamin (3) have three tins each with labels marked, Give, Save and Spend. Their pocket money is given in small change—it delights my heart that they choose to put half of it in the Give tin!

So we can see that the implications of this command are far reaching. It isn't just a prohibition on walking into a shop and taking something, but concerns a far more fundamental attitude. An attitude which sees everything we have been given as a gift, something we are responsible for. Property is not wrong, but we have a tremendous obligation in all that we do to be respon-

sible, to be honest, to look not only to our interests.
Again and again I have thought how radically transformed society would be if there was no stealing, how
work relationships, communities, friendships, economic policy would be changed. We don't want simply
to dream of an impossible utopia, but to provide a
stimulus that things don't have to be the way they are.
They can change. And that change can start with us!

You shall not commit adultery.
Exodus 20:14

As we approach the end of the twentieth century many things about ourselves and our world are still a puzzle. There is still the search for the right way to run a country's affairs. Numerous diseases flummox our best doctors. There are still new pieces of historical evidence coming to light on events in the past. There is a growing search for meaning as we face the twenty-first century and contemporary culture tries to work out what it stands for and what it holds dear. Among all this, one thing is for certain: we are preoccupied with sex. Not preoccupied with love, with caring, with relationships; but with sex. The late Malcolm Muggeridge said, 'I've got sex on the brain and it's the worst place to have it!' Sex is used to sell cars, holidays, clothes, perfume, coffee and toothpaste. It is the main refrain of nearly all popular music. It is the subject of many films, plays and best-selling books. It is not romance that we are interested in, it is not commitment that we are sold by the media; it is purely and simply—pleasure. Feelings are what rule. 'If it feels good, do it', and that is the only rule.

We live in a society where the 'feel good factor' is the

driving principle. Pleasure is the name and goal of the game. Hedonism (the pursuit of pleasure) is the philosophy. The driving questions are not, 'What is truth?' or 'What is real?', but, 'What feels good?' Sex is the most travelled route to the kingdom of pleasure, but along its path lie bodies trampled underfoot. We are sold the lie that the sexual act is really just like a physical erotic game of squash. Intercourse is merely a physical act of pleasure which holds no other ties than creating a hunger for more.

The whole preoccupation with sex isn't just a characteristic of our generation; all peoples of all times have had an obsession with sex. A glance at Greek culture, Indian art or even Shakespeare's plays shows this. And it was obviously an issue for the people of Israel over 3,000 years ago. God showed them that he cared and was concerned about the way in which they conducted their sexual relations. And the God of the Ten Commandments is the same God as today. He does not change; neither do his ways and commands. This Commandment has stood as relevant to every culture in every generation in every age. That is why God gave it.

But the standards of this age are quickly becoming not only different from God's, but in direct conflict with them. A recent survey in one of the leading men's fashion magazines in the country proclaimed with great joy as absolute fact their research had found that 73 per cent of men could have sex *with no emotional ties*. It is not that I contest the figures as being too high or too low, or that they are not actually a fair reflection of what people really believe. It's that the question is a non-starter; there is no such thing as having sexual intercourse without implications and that is why we have the Seventh Commandment.

More than 85 per cent of adults marry at some time in their lives and those people hope that their marriages will last. In a recent survey almost nine out of ten of those interviewed said that they valued faithfulness as the most important ingredient in marriage.

There is little doubt that as we approach the end of the twentieth century marriage faces a crisis. It won't do simply to wax lyrical about a bygone age when all was blissful as regards family life and marriage, because research shows that that time never really existed except in the romantic memories of some. The facts of the matter are that today marriage is facing a crisis point.

Although fewer people are getting married, marriage still remains popular. In Britain the latest estimates are that over 50 per cent of all marriages will end in divorce. Half of the divorces come from marriages which lasted less than ten years. The most common cause of divorce is *adultery*.

One survey showed that 51 per cent of divorced men who have not remarried wished they had stayed with their former partner and among those who had remarried the proportion is 37 per cent. An increasing proportion of marriages are remarriages. Over a third (36 per cent) of all marriages involve at least one partner who has been married before and in 17 per cent of weddings, both the bride and groom have been married before. A higher proportion of second marriages end in divorce. Current trends suggest one in two marriages involving a partner married before ends in divorce.

Most divorces involve children. Some 55 per cent of all divorces in 1988 involved children under the age of sixteen, and 150,000 children under sixteen are caught up in divorces every year. The majority of children are under ten years old. Every week 2,900 children are involved in their parents' divorce. Of these 940, or a third, are under the age of five and another 1,160 are between the ages of five and ten. One in five children can expect to experience the divorce of their parents before the age of sixteen. It is projected that by 1996 50 per cent of children will be born to couples who won't be together after the child is sixteen.

Divorce does have an effect on children. Delinquency is twice as high among young people who experienced their parents' divorce while they were under the age of five. Women are more likely to divorce if their parents' marriage ended while they were less than five years old. Children who experience their parents' divorce during their school years are more likely to have a lower educational attainment and men at the age of eighteen are more likely to be unemployed.

But the cost borne in terms of human suffering is far more than we can ever comprehend through statistics. When a nation lowers its sexual standards of behaviour, we build into ourselves the seeds of our own destruction. As our families fragment, so do the deepest structures of our society. When a family breaks down, so do the values which once linked parents and children and gave community and character to our changing world.

Because choice is one of the gods of this age and hedonism another, some of the concepts of family run against these. For example, to be a husband or wife is to accept the exclusion of other sexual relationships. Rabbi Jonathan Sacks said in the 1990 Reith Lectures that 'our current lack of norms relating to sexuality and marriage precisely reflects the supreme importance we have given to the·abstract individual, without a binding commitment either to the past or to the long-term future, open-endedly free to choose or unchoose any style of life'. The upshot is that 'the family has lost its moral base. Adultery, the most selfish expression of free choice may bring short-term pleasure for a night, but it brings long-term misery to all involved, the participants, those close to those involved and the wider community. We cannot overestimate the effect on this society and the society our children will inherit.'

Of all the behaviour that can attack marriage, adultery is the one recognised as the most serious. Adultery can vary from a casual fling to the deep, personal involvement when an affair becomes a permanent relationship. The intense, long drawn out triangle which films, magazines and novels glamorise is in real life exceedingly painful and stressful. Some people numb their consciences. Others find it all a great amusement and proudly brag about their latest affair or conquest. Others continue an adulterous affair out of apathy, convenience or fear of offending their lovers and the possible ramifications if the private relationship became public knowledge. Others are locked in an unhappy marriage, seeking solace elsewhere because they see no hope of improving things at home. In her book,

Intimate Partners, Maggie Scarfe insists that what is learnt in an affair can be brought back into marriage, enriching and enhancing it. 'A three-legged table,' she says, 'is obviously easier to keep in a balanced state than a two-legged table.' In an article in *The Guardian* in August 1994, Liz Bircham, a Relate counsellor replied to this opinion, 'I have yet to come across a case in which a third party enhanced a relationship.'

If I were to walk into a main shopping street and ask what the general public thought the Bible's view of sex was, there is little doubt most of the feedback would be negative. It is true that in the past Christianity has been guilty of putting up a dividing wall between things of the 'body' being bad and negative and things of the 'soul' being good and positive. But that is not a biblical view. God is not indifferent to what we are or do physically. He made us physical beings with all our humanness and fleshliness. He made us with our senses, with our needs for food and drink, with our need for intimacy and relationships within our community and with our desire for sexual intimacy and fulfilment with each other. It is because God has such a positive view of our sexuality, it is because he has such a high regard for sexual intimacy and fulfilment that he gave this Commandment.

In the very first chapter of the Bible God affirms in the beings of his creation the sexual desire: 'Be fruitful and multiply and fill the earth.' God formed Eve to stand with Adam and the two individuals became one. 'Therefore shall a man leave his father and his mother and shall cleave unto his wife, and they shall become one flesh' (Genesis 2:24 AV). This statement is repeated four times in the rest of the Bible. The emphasis is clear that in marriage God intends a man and a woman to find sexual fulfilment in a one-to-one lifelong monogamous relationship. Therefore any act of sexual intercourse out of that monogamous lifelong relationship, either with another partner after the lifelong commitment has been made, or before that point is reached, falls short of the ideal that God has set for humanity.

Within that lifelong commitment, sex is a gift of God to the couple to express their intimacy and delight with one another and their 'one-ness'. It is there that sexual fulfilment is truly found. And far from having a negative view of sexual intercourse, the Bible actually raves about this act of love. One whole book of the Bible, Song of Songs, is a love song between two lovers. Sex is great but only in its proper context. Dr David Field in his book, *God's Good Life* (IVP 1992) gives a helpful analogy:

> Glue is great, but only for sticking things together. Use it to give yourself an artificial 'high' and you are abusing it. Sex is meant for sticking people together in the tight bond of marriage. But having sex outside marriage is using a good thing in the wrong way. So adultery is the sexual equivalent of solvent abuse.

But what is the Bible's understanding of marriage?

Whenever Jesus was questioned about marriage or adultery, he always went back to the accounts of creation to remind his listeners of the perfect standard God laid down when he first breathed life into man and woman, quoting Genesis 2:24. It is worth looking at it again: 'Therefore a man will leave his father and mother and cleave to his wife and they will become one flesh.' Jesus is making three clear statements about marriages: leaving, cleaving and one flesh.

Marriage corresponds to these three things:

- The legal, social responsibility—*leave*
- The personal, emotional commitment—*cleave*
- The physical union—*one flesh*

These three aspects constitute marriage in God's sight. The reason that adultery is so serious is that it breaks into the unity that two people have in marriage.

Leave

'A man will leave his father and mother.'

God recognises that other people will be involved. The new couple set up a new family unit and build a new home—it is a statement to the rest of society that from that time on the two are not to be seen as separate individuals by the community, but as an entity in themselves. But marriage is not simply a contract. The two parties do not draw up a contract of conditions which must be kept; it is not about bargaining; it is not focused on things but on a new life together; it is more than a licence to start a family; it is more than a romantic alliance; it is as the Bible says a *covenant*.

Covenant means more than a legal contract; it is a binding promise to be in a special relationship only with the person on the other side of the covenant. This is what marriage is, not a contract but a covenant, and the first way that is shown is by leaving the status that once one belonged to as a single person before one entered the covenant relationship and becoming something different after the covenant service.

It is becoming more and more common for couples to co-habit. This may be as a trial for marriage—the old line being that you can only get to know someone when you have lived with them and you should only marry someone you really know, hence you can only really know if you want to marry someone after you have lived with them. Some people may believe that marriage is outdated, or feel that they honestly are not ready to make the lifelong commitment to each other that marriage requires and so settle for the short-term option of living together until they are at that point, or until they realise that they will never be at that point. Today, nearly half the couples who get married have previously lived together. And over 70 per cent of divorced men and women live with their future partner prior to remarriage.

This is a very complex issue. I think it is enough to say here that Christianity requires that for marriage a public ceremony is held in which the two individuals come together in front of society and by their own declaration are recognised to be setting themselves apart for one another from that moment on in a way in which they hadn't done or been previously. So there is a time the night before the ceremony when they are not married and a time twenty-four hours later when it can be said that they are married because they have gone through a public ceremony from which their status in the community and the wider society has changed.

Cleave

The Hebrew word actually means 'to glue'. It is a good analogy as we have already seen. If you glue two pieces of paper together and later try and tear them apart, you do not tear the glue, you tear the paper. This is exactly what happens in separation.

In the marriage service vows are made in the name of God. There is no promise to maintain the marriage so long as romantic love feelings are still there, but to 'love and to cherish till death us do part'. This love is not simply something of the head and the heart, but of the will. That is why we are asked, 'Will you promise?' We cannot promise with romantic or erotic love. However we can promise with the love talked about here because it is modelled on God's love for us and God's love is based on his will towards us. It is something he decides. In a marriage ceremony the decision by the two people for one another is declared and promised:

> For better, for worse,
> For richer, for poorer,
> In sickness and in health,
> To love and to cherish
> Till death us do part,
> According to God's holy law
> And this is my solemn vow.

In the sixties the contemporary American poet Rod McKuen came up with a version of the marriage service for his own generation. Set in a beautiful forest glade the couple say the following vows to each other:

I believe in love. I believe the person I will walk away with today to start another lifetime with to be someone I wish to comfort and I will expect comfort in return. I will share everything I have to share, I will always expect the sharing and giving returned.

The 'minister' then says:

This is a vow forever. If forever should end for the two of you, or one of you, tomorrow or next year, stay together only as long as you need one another. Go only when your need for the other person ends.

What a fascinating expression of partnership. But we cannot do just that.

Many people really believe they have done the same on their marriage vows. They might have said outwardly that they would be faithful but in effect they meant that they would stay, but not that they would be entirely faithful. If you read many of the interviews with those who are being unfaithful in marriage you would find that many have rationalised their adultery in such a way as to let them continue to believe that they have not broken their marriage vows, because they are just unable to live with the daily reality that they have breached the marriage covenant. Now we just cannot do that. We see the farce of that sixties marriage service, because for ever cannot mean whatever length of time I want it to mean; for ever *means* for ever.

Language expresses something; we cannot just put into it any meaning we want. It is a characteristic of our post-modern society that it allows people to do all sorts of things with language; we can give language whatever meaning we want, ascribing our own interpretation when we use a certain word or giving our own meaning when we make a certain promise. Some people even do the same with language about God, publicly declaring the ancient historical creeds and then saying, 'I actually put my own interpretation on that, and what I really mean is . . .' and come out with something which is completely contrary to what they have just said. We are called to integrity in our language, and the language of the marriage service is unequivocal in its meaning. It's a promise 'until death do us part'.

In English we use the word 'love' to mean so many things that we never really know for sure what we are talking about. The Greeks had no such problems because they had four different words for love.

The first word is 'Philia' which means friendship and companionship, the emotional sharing of time and interests; it shows a desire to co-operate.

The second is the word 'Storge' which means affection, good-will, concern and kindness. This is the kind of love we show to our elders, to young children; it is active care.

The third word is 'Eros', the root of the word erotic, the love that seeks sensual expression.

The fourth word 'Agape' means a love which comes from the realisation and understanding of the worth and preciousness of the person. This is the way God loves us; the character and quality of this love is determined by the character of God. Agape love is a selfless, total giving love.

It is obviously essential that all four types of love are

present and expressed in the marriage relationship, but it is this agape love, the one we are told about in the Bible, with which we are to love our marriage partner. For this is the love that God has for you and me. The only security I have that God my Father will not fall out of love with me is that he never fell in love with me. There was never a time when I wasn't loved by him. We are to reflect the nature of our Creator. Agape love holds a marriage together.

We often hear those who are experiencing marital breakdown say, 'I just don't love them any more.' Is it 'don't' or 'won't'? Is it not we can't or won't? God says we can wilfully agape.

One flesh

One of the contradictions of our society is its view of sex. On the one hand we are persuaded by the world around us that we value sex more than any other society or generation. We are the generation who are sexually free and liberated. We are the ones who can be fully sexually fulfilled. In the past it was taught that to resist one's instinct was to go against nature; now we know differently. And we apparently show our high view of sex by singing about it, by making films about it, by writing books full of passionate scenes, by screening soap opera after soap opera revolving round various sexual liaisons. Our best-selling newspapers are the ones whose pages contain the most about sex.

And yet as we triumphantly parade our sexual liberation and fulfilment we probably experience more failed relationships, more broken lives, more abuse, more perversion, more stories which fill us with horror, disgust and sickness. It leads us to ask ourselves, 'What is the world coming to . . . ?' And we realise that our society, which has turned sexuality into the biggest factor in selling, actually betrays a lower view of sex than at any other time in our known history.

People who enjoy the short-term pleasure end up broken and spent, realising they are less fulfilled than when they began their search. What was it a search for? They at first kidded themselves it was just a search for pleasure, but deep down they know it was a search for love, for acceptance, to feel valuable, to feel worth, quite simply to be loved. And the voices which shout at the church that it's behind the times, that it simply represses human sexuality, that it doesn't allow for sexual fulfilment, that it's stuck in the Dark Ages, have a very hollow ring to them. Because this so-called high view of sex has brought them only short-term cheap thrills, it has sold them short, it has not delivered; it has turned out to have the lowest view of human beings ever, reducing them simply to animal instinct, to objects of pleasure, creating mistrust, fear, betrayal, despair, hurt, and fatal diseases.

Contrary to popular opinion, God does not have a low view of sex. In fact he has the highest view—that is that sexual intercourse is the final act of complete self-giving and appropriate only to the special relationship of two people, male and female, becoming one with each other. As God made one man for one woman, the true intimacy of sexual intercourse should only be expressed within a loving monogamous life-long relationship.

Becoming one flesh is an act of complete self-giving, on both sides of the partnership.

Sex does not make love; love makes sex. It is an act of expression of love and commitment. The Bible says that sexual relations can never be merely a casual affair. A oneness exists which produces an identity of flesh. Such a union flows over into the whole being of the persons involved and cannot be limited to a surface entanglement soon to be forgotten.

This Commandment is given to us by God that we might know what ways we are to express the sexuality that God has placed in us. He made us as sexual beings and therefore knows how we best work. The only long-term way of sexual fulfilment is with one person for life. God does not leave us to work this out on our own. He tells us in this command. This Commandment brings freedom. I don't know anyone who has adhered to it who has regretted it, but nearly everyone I know who has broken it wished they hadn't!

You shall not murder.
Exodus 20:23

There are few news items that horrify us more than news of a particularly gruesome murder. We are moved to revulsion when we read or hear of men and women who have caused such painful and cruel deaths to others. The mandatory sentence for murder is life-imprisonment. The most notorious criminals of this generation have been those who have killed in horrific and callous ways: the Yorkshire Ripper, the Moors Murderers and serial killers. We may think this Commandment holds no problems for us; surely all of us would agree that murder is wrong. All decent societies uphold that; no one in their right mind could possibly oppose the logic of the Sixth Commandment.

Here we are concerned with social order in the community and we see clearly illustrated the fact that the Commandments are not simply nice ideas, suggestions or good advice, not just insights into what might be the best choice to make in a particular situation, not even prescriptions for a happy social life. These commands are instructions which our society ignores at its peril.

But if we leave this command thinking it is simply

about the crime of murder we miss its relevance to our everyday life as a society and as separate persons within the community. Let's look deeper into this whole area of 'life' raised by this Commandment.

On the one hand . . .

Medical science does its upmost to preserve and enhance life. Those who work in the caring professions battle each day to maintain life and to put off death for as long as possible. Some of the advances in medical science are truly amazing as breakthrough after breakthrough offers hope to those who just one hundred years ago would not have had any hope in the face of their disease or injury. From vaccination to organ transplants, from chemotherapy to intensive care for premature babies, our health service has a dramatic effect on the lifespan of many people. All these things show how highly we value life and how much we want to live and want those who are nearest and dearest to us, and those whom we do not know to live. Life is the most precious gift we know of.

In the last few decades there has been a growing awareness of injustices that go on within the borders of other countries: human rights abuse, torture, imprisonment for political belief or religious practice. Groups such as Amnesty International have done a vital job alerting the West about many of the injustices which happen in other parts of the world and on its own doorstep. Public outcry in the international community and through pressure groups has caused nations to realise that life has to be respected, and long may this continue. For there are still many parts of the world where men and women, children and babies suffer for their race, their beliefs, their ethnic background or simply from being in the wrong place at the wrong time. The horror we feel at such stories and events rightly leads us to affirm the inherent worth of human life, that each person has a right to live, which should not be taken away from them; but more than that no one else has a right to take that life away. That, we feel, is God's prerogative.

On the other hand . . .

In this century some 9,700,000 people perished in World War One and the toll in World War Two is estimated to be around 55 million. Over 6 million Jews were exterminated by the policy of Adolf Hitler because they were deemed to be 'racially degenerate' and therefore expendable. Since 1945, over 26 million people have died in war.

In Holland it is now legal for a person's life to be terminated by their own wish or the wishes of their family; the right to end one's life is declared as a legal prerogative of each person.

Some medical students were attending a seminar on abortion. The lecturer faced them with a case study. 'The father of the family has syphilis and the mother TB. They have four children already. The first is blind, the second died, the third deaf and dumb and the fourth has TB. The mother is now pregnant with her fifth child and is willing to have an abortion if that is what you suggest. What would your advice be?' The students voted by a majority that the pregnancy should be terminated. 'Congratulations,' commented the lecturer. 'You have just wiped out Beethoven.'

Each year in the UK an increased number of foetuses are aborted. Usually the cry is that it is the woman's right to choose what to do with her own body and her own future so Parliament simply amended a Bill which was drafted to reduce the time limit on abortions, and increased it to the highest level in Europe.

As Joy Davidman says in her book, *Smoke on the Mountain*, 'No previous age has ever equalled the horror of killing, but then no previous age has ever killed so much.'

Most people think that God gave us his command because in any human society you can't have people taking human life indiscriminately. And that is obviously true as far as it goes. But far more fundamental to this is the perspective that God gives, that he has given life to us, who are made in his image and we are not in the position of authority to take it away.

So what does this Commandment mean for us today?

There are two fundamental assumptions which this Commandment rests on.

Life comes from God and belongs to God

All life is God's gift. God is the author and giver of life. He is the only one who is able to give life. We read in the first book of the Bible that God made humans and 'breathed life into them'. God is the only one who has the power to give life and he is the only one who has the right to take it away. Medical advances have been huge in the last few years, especially in the whole area of birth. But the one thing which is completely unachievable by science is the creation of life, to create a living organism. Only God can give life and each life is a gift from him.

Many people up and down the country confront me with the question, 'What has God ever done for me?' Well, where do you start? Let's start at the beginning of your life shall we, or somewhere closer to home? What about this morning, when you woke up and found yourself alive? Who do you think gave you that life? Who gave you that breath?

To regard human lives as expendable, as pawns in a game that we can get rid of whenever they pose an inconvenience to us, to regard the death of other human beings as of little consequence, ignores the intrinsic value of the human being.

Philosophers love posing dilemmas. Here's one. You're standing there in the National Gallery at the opening of an art exhibition. Suddenly a fire breaks out and spreads with enormous speed. In front of you is a priceless Leonardo. To your right is your four-year-old daughter. Which do you save? If you emerged into the light with the painting, the 'arty' types might be grateful, but we really know there's no dilemma here at all. You save the life. Because people matter more than things. Because a God-given life is the most valuable thing in the world, people all over the world will do everything possible to prolong life. For this reason we find moving stories of men and women giving their own lives for the sake of someone else, whether it be rescuers who go into burning flames to rescue people and sacrifice their own lives, or fathers who drown saving the lives of their own children, or stories of people in a concentration camp who gave up their own lives in place of others. All these examples of selfless-ness move us because we realise they are giving up everything they have. Jesus said the same:

> No one has greater love than this: to lay down his life for his friends.
>
> John 15:13 MLB

We are not the creators of life; God is. Life comes from God and belongs to him.

Men and women are made in the image of God

The Bible says the distinguishing mark of all humans is that we are made in the image of God. The Creator has stamped and formed human beings uniquely with his own likeness.

> So God created mankind in his own image, in the image of God he created them, male and female he created them.
>
> Genesis 1:27

This does not mean that we look physically like God! It does mean that characteristics that we have—the capacity to love, to make moral choices, etc., are mirrors of God's character. But, more than that, God is a God who relates. And it is in this way that we are made in his image. We are made to relate to him and to each other in loving relationships.

The Bible carries throughout its pages the assumption that it is not enough simply to say that killing equals murder. So it seems important at this point to state what this Commandment is not about.

It is not about the killing of animals.

It is not about accidental killing. We know this because there are other laws in the Old Testament which explain what happens when an accident has occurred which has ended in someone's death.

It is not about capital punishment. Now the whole Bible tells us something about the intrinsic value of human life, but it is obvious that this Commandment was not seen as an instruction to Hebrew society not to enforce the death penalty. Whether we like it or not, Hebrew society did enforce the death penalty. Now I happen to believe from the rest of the Bible, especially in the light of Jesus' teaching, and looking at the effects of capital punishment, that it would be a retrograde step for a society to uphold a policy of capital punishment. But I'm well aware that this is an issue where there is disagreement. Although this command says something about God's value upon human life, which needs to be taken into account when we are thinking through issues such as the death penalty, it does not say everything on the subject.

It is not pacifism. As we have already noted, the sense of this command is not, 'You shall not kill.' If it really did mean that, it would be pretty strange that the reaction of the Hebrew people wasn't to turn into a pacifist people. They certainly didn't. Once again we are touching on a very large and complex debate, which I am not going to deal with here. It will suffice to say that the 'just war' theory was developed in the Christian church in the Middle Ages to try and work out what might be the way forward as regards war and the intrinsic value of human life. Such decisions are not easy ones, but it does seem wise and necessary to provide some framework in which people and communities can weigh up the possibility of resistance and defence, and the 'just war' theory goes a long way to meeting that. Jesus forbade his followers from taking up arms to defend him.

But there are dilemmas that men and women face. Dietrich Bonhoeffer was a young German minister when Adolf Hitler was elected to power in Germany in the 1930s. He and a small minority of the church were horrified by Hitler's rise and actively opposed him and the State's control of the church, becoming known as the 'Confessing Church'. In the mid-thirties the pacifist Bonhoeffer was working in London, but decided that it was his Christian duty to return to Germany and oppose Hitler. The way in which he felt it right to do this was by joining a bomb-plot to kill Hitler, and so eradicate the evil dictator. While the bomb-plot was underway, he was arrested on charges of conspiracy, and the attempt on Hitler's life failed. He was held in prison for a long time and was executed in 1945. His death inspired subsequent generations of Christians who seek to know the legitimate response to two evils. His was not a choice he was particularly proud of, but it was the one which he believed was the lesser of two evils, and he believed it fell to him to sacrifice his life to try and provide something—not for himself, but for subsequent generations.

We have looked at what this Commandment is not about. Now let us focus our attention on two dilemmas which we face on which this Commandment does have some bearing.

Abortion

We have already commented on the immensely high abortion figures in this country, which many of us find particularly worrying.

I want to say to those of you who are reading this and feel crippled inside because you have actually had an abortion, please turn to God who forgives, who can heal your feelings and regrets. You do not have to earn forgiveness. In fact you cannot; all you can do is to acknowledge and express your regret to God and know that he is more than willing to forgive. It would probably help if you read some of the parts of the Bible which deal with forgiveness: Psalm 51, Psalm 103: 8–12, Romans 5:2, 2 Corinthians 5: 16–21 and 1 John 1: 8–9.

The big debate often centres around when exactly the child's life begins. A sperm has twenty-three chromosomes, an egg also has twenty-three chromosomes; on fertilisation they become one cell with forty-six chromosomes. From that one cell will develop a human being, with a God-given life and made in the image of God.

The difficulty is in saying when the human life is different from the potential of human life, or whether the two things are different, as some would like us to think. There is much talk of the 'woman's right to choose', but what about the baby's right to life?

By the time a foetus is eighteen days old—which is long before the mother is sure she is pregnant—the heart is already beating. At forty-five days an electro-encephalographic receiver can pick up waves from the baby's developing brain. By twelve weeks a baby has fingernails, sucks its thumb and can recoil from pain. By the fourth month, the baby is eight to ten inches in height. The fifth month is the time of lengthening and strengthening—skin and hair grow. The baby then begins to respond to light and sound. In this country it is legal to have an abortion up to twenty-four weeks into the pregnancy.

This whole issue is very emotive and complex because it involves human life. Personally I believe that abortion is allowable in two instances only. First, to stop pregnancy following a rape. Secondly, when a mother's life will be lost if the abortion does not take place. This is my personal opinion and it is not for me to dictate to you. I have presented you with the facts of developing life and would plead that as individuals and society we consider the possibility of terminating a life in the light of God's Commandment.

It is, I believe, important that we offer care, support and advice, practical and financial help to those women who are in the agonising position of facing an unwanted pregnancy. We cannot just proclaim our stance and retreat. If we are going to hold high values on this issue which I believe we should, we are also going to have to put our money where our mouth is.

This will mean we welcome those single mothers who have made the difficult decision to have their child, and not be seen to look down our noses at them. We need to be as practically loving as we are firm.

Euthanasia

The literal meaning of the word euthanasia is 'dying well', but the term has come to mean intentional killing of a patient by a doctor under specified circumstances.

As far as this country is concerned, thanks to the brilliant work of some Christians, it is not likely that Parliament will legalise euthanasia in the near future. Those who favour 'voluntary euthanasia' believe that in a significant number of cases the only way to ensure a peaceful and dignified death is for the doctor to be given the right to end the patient's life. There have been a number of very complex and controversial cases recently in which certain actions by doctors have been under review. For as the English law now stands, this constitutes murder.

It is important to distinguish euthanasia from two practices with which it is sometimes confused. The first is allowing a patient who is suffering from a fatal disease to die in peace without being subjected to troublesome treatments which cannot restore them to health. The second is the use of pain-killing drugs to control severe pain even at the risk of shortening life. These are now generally accepted by the medical profession and raise no problems of moral principle. The purpose here is to provide a peaceful and dignified environment in which people can end their life on this earth. However it should be stressed that there is often a struggle with knowing whether intervention will help or hinder a patient, both physically and emotionally.

When it comes to euthanasia, however, one of the problems is that those who are the oldest in society, the ones in pain, those who take a lot of looking after, are just done away with rather than providing them with a dignified and respectful way to end their lives. If euthanasia were to be legalised one would have to be concerned that unscrupulous families who stand much to gain materially from the will of an elderly relative could put undue pressure on that relative to agree to euthanasia before their time was up. Also, those elderly people who fear becoming a burden to their families or friends might feel that it would be better for everyone if they ceased to be a drain on resources. The emphasis on people's right to die takes too little account of the ties that bind people to one another and encourages the sick, the terminally ill, and the elderly to regard themselves as easily disposable.

This is not how God sees them. So this command of not murdering plays a huge part in how we should endeavour to build our society. However carefully a law was drafted, in practice it would be impossible to avoid abuse or to draw a line clearly between cases which the law considered justified and those which it did not.

We should heed what God says:

I put to death and I bring to life.

Deuteronomy 32:39

But what about our everyday lives? We have seen how this command might be a basis for right and just laws in our society, but Jesus doesn't leave this Commandment there; this is what he says in the Sermon on the Mount:

> You have heard that it was said to those of ancient times, 'You shall not murder', and 'Whoever murders shall be liable to judgement'. But I say to you that if you are angry with a brother or sister you will be liable to judgement; and if you insult a brother or sister, you will be liable to the Council.

Matthew 5:21–22 NRSV

Just when people had thought that they didn't have a problem with this command, Jesus brings a new perspective. Jesus is not saying here that it is wrong to get angry. He can't be saying that for the simple reason that we see throughout the Bible that God becomes angry when he sees people doing things wrong. It is righteous anger which comes from his love. It is not an anger which seeks to destroy and punish for the sake of it; rather it is an anger which burns against injustice because of what it does to the people God gave life to and made in his image. Jesus himself got angry at the money changers and traders in the Temple who were using the house of God to make profits. Anger is not wrong. In fact, it is absolutely right that we get angry when we see brutal injustice or hear stories of oppression or cruelty. The problem with anger comes when it is destructive, when it burns inside and eats us up, when it seeks to get even. That sort of anger Jesus says is tantamount to murder. Wishing evil on someone, wanting them to suffer, is not a right way to react in a situation. It amounts to wanting them murdered and one of Jesus' hardest sayings was that what goes on in our thoughts is as important to God as what we actually do.

We are all aware of times and occasions when we have harboured anger and hurt in our hearts and minds. We have wasted so much creative energy on how we might get even or how we might pay them back for what they have done to us. We have held private 'pity-parties' for ourselves to wallow in our own self-pity, but have ended up even more morose at the end of it, even more full of our own grievances. We have become bitter, which has affected everything and everyone else around us. Medical knowledge is clear that bitterness has a serious effect on the health of the one who harbours it.

So Jesus goes on to tell those listening that when they go to worship God, and remember that they are not in a good relationship with someone else, they must first put that relationship right. We have the opportunity to go and put our relationships right with one another. If there is someone whom I have fallen out with, whom I am angry at, I must go and make peace with that person. It matters to God how we treat one another. Because all life is a gift from him and every man, woman and child bears his image. People must be respected.

What goes on inside people's hearts and minds has an effect on how they act. Jesus again said, '. . . it is from within, from the human heart, that evil intentions come: fornication, theft, murder, adultery . . .' (Mark 7:21–22). Jesus' brother James says the same thing in his letter:

What causes wars, and what causes fightings among you?
Is it not your passions that are at war in your members?
You desire and do not have; so you kill.

James 4:1–2 RSV

We cannot simply point the finger at the people we
want behind bars because of this Commandment.
Because that points at our violence of feeling and
action. Again, Joy Davidman says, 'Few of us would
actually murder our neighbour. But can we acquit ourselves of those offences which our Lord compared to
murder?' If this world could only grasp the power of
forgiveness. Being able to forgive someone breaks the
cycle of bitterness and vengeance.

And before us are not just empty words of Jesus, but
his life. Jesus practised what he preached. He tells his
followers that they must not hate their enemies, but
love them. And he did just that at a time when we
might think he had the most right to curse, to call
down judgement, to hate those who were crucifying
him. Instead he prayed for their forgiveness. We are
called to follow a God who doesn't impose his rules at
us from above, but has lived them.

This Commandment affirms to every person in this
world that they are of intrinsic value to God. He will
not tolerate the taking of life by murder, he will not
tolerate even the hatred that is the first step down the
path to murder. He is the God of life who showed his
commitment to us, who showed us the full extent of
the value he places on our life by giving his own life.

Honour your father and mother, so that you may live long in the land the Lord your God is giving you.
Exodus 20:12

Few things give us as much pleasure in life as our families.

Few things give as much pain in life as our families!

We all have different experiences of families, but on the whole, each of us has both good and bad memories. In this Commandment we see that God cares about our home situations.

Read any teenage magazine and you will see story after story of problems with parents. Listen in on any conversation between parents and you will sense the worry and fear of their children becoming wayward. Sometimes such anxieties are very real, sometimes it is good to talk things through with contemporaries to get advice. But it all betrays a divide between parent and child. This conflict between parent and child, child and parent, seems real and very important. Indeed it not only seems to be so, it is.

Life is full of this tension between the generations. Some of them are quite humorous, some are devastating and agonisingly serious. Think of the conflicts which are raised in the following situations:

Conventional fathers whose sons grow their hair long and have their ears pierced.

Mothers whose daughters grow up to be more attractive than them.

Students who have opportunities in education their parents never had and who become much more educated than them.

Elderly grandparents who become more and more dependent on others and who fear becoming an imposition on the family.

Fathers whose daughters become higher wage-earners than they are.

Mothers whose sons marry someone they think is unsuitable.

Sons who are never quite able to live up to their father's expectations.

Daughters who are never quite trusted or let go of by their fathers.

Children who are expected to live near home but desperately want to move away and live their own life.

Sons and daughters who become Christians in direct opposition to their parents.

Children whose parents divorce acrimoniously and have to decide who to live with.

Children with a single parent who goes through a whole host of other partners.

None of the above scenarios is far-fetched. I would suggest that each of us is personally familiar with some of these or is aware of people who fit nearly all of these categories.

This Commandment teaches us something about

our responsibility to our families in every situation. This Commandment was given to the families of the Israelites who lived in a very different setting than we have today. The families were bigger and didn't just consist of parents and children. Rather, they were extended families with grandparents, fathers, mothers, children, grandchildren with aunts, uncles and cousins living just in the next tent. It was very close. You didn't grow up and go off to college. You didn't grow up and decide what your job was going to be. You did what your father did if you were a male, and if you were a female you accepted the role laid down for you. This was non-negotiable; you didn't have a choice because it just didn't exist. This was the way it was. It was not something imprisoning, it was something that was freeing; the family gave nurture and support; it was the place for education and learning; it was the source of livelihood and provision. Everything centred on the family unit. Families stuck together. Land, housing, education, wealth and job were all tied in with the family. Children were assets; the importance of the family could not be overestimated.

That is true throughout the Bible. Genesis begins with the story of the first family and tells the stories of many other families: Noah's, Abraham and Sarah's, Jacob and Rebekah's. The context for so many stories is in the family. Rabbi Jonathan Sacks suggests that 'the survival of the Jewish people throughout almost 4000 years of exile and dispersion is due above all to the strength of its families'.

King David, the Bible's most respected and important king, had one main weakness—he couldn't control his own family. So there were numerous *coups d'état* as various of his rebellious sons tried to take the throne. The role one played in the family was as important, if not more important, than the role one played in society. Family life was vital.

But today we are all aware that the family unit has undergone major batterings and is in danger of being irreversibly changed. Some herald this as a good thing and will only rest when the family as a social unit is abolished. Karl Marx suggested that the bourgeois family lay at the heart of the oppressive capitalist economy. Radical post-Freudians argue that it is a source of psychological distress. Feminists like Shulamith Firestone have seen it as the perpetration of the patriarchy. And Sir Edmund Leach summed it up when he said, 'Far from being the basis of the good society, the family with its narrow privacy and tawdry secrets, is the source of all discontents.'

I disagree with all the above. The family is not just one of our institutions, but *the* formative one. God cares about the way our families are structured, the way they work, the way they are set up, the way in which we relate to one another within them and the way in which we treat each other within them. And so he gave us this command.

It is in this century that the family has undergone the most significant and potentially straining changes. We need to be aware of what these are so we can work out what it means to honour our father and mother today.

One of the new creations of this century, which no other century has had, is the teenager. The term arose in America after the Second World War and was used to describe the young people coming through adolescence and puberty into maturity. It is now not only a term used to describe certain years of life, it describes a whole mindset, a whole world view, an attitude towards life. To be a teenager is not necessarily to be in your teens.

Since the 1950s youth culture has revolved around the fact that teenagers looking for involvement, craving for responsibility and wanting to be taken seriously, have been denied all these things by the adult world. At all times in previous history, all cultures have offered to their adolescent children responsibility around the age of puberty. This is true in the case of the ancient Israelites to whom this Commandment was first given.

As well as the physical changes at this age, there are the psychological, spiritual and intellectual changes. It is the dawn of a new stage in their lives; independence is looming on the horizon and they want it *now*!

Too often it is called rebellion. Parents up and down western countries denounce the actions of their teenage children as sheer revolution against the way they were brought up, because their children start dressing differently, listening to different music, pursuing different interests and basically asserting their differences and independence at every possible opportunity. But it is not fresh-faced rebellion for the sake of it. It's the same way as in nature a young bird will reach the stage where it has a natural desire to fly the nest. Teenagers are simply expressing the desire to fly the nest themselves. They want to be their own people, have some meaning to their lives and to make some

difference to the world. So there is this tension, this
conflict where they yearn for responsibility and yet it
will not be given to them.

In the western world society has changed so much
that what was the norm for adolescence in the last
century is no longer the case now. Western culture has
taken away the responsibility that was given in previous
generations and is still given in other cultures. This
leaves teens powerless.

Music has been a phenomenon which has allowed
teenagers to create some expression of their own.
They have been shut out of things too long, having
no responsibility, no place in society except to wait
until they are adults. So popular culture gives them
the opportunity to create their own world, with their
own values and their own meaning. They can dress in
the clothes they want to, listen to the music which
only people like them listen to. And the more the
adults hate it, the more it belongs to them. It is their
own.

> The world is passing through troubled times. Young
> people of today think of nothing but themselves. They
> have no respect for parents or old age. They are impatient
> of all restraint. They talk as if they know everything, and
> treat our wisdom as stupidity. As for girls, they are
> forward, immodest and unwomanly in speech and behav-
> iour.

When do you think that was written? This decade? In
the sixties more likely? At the turn of the century? Well,
last century then? No. It was written in the year
AD 1274 by Peter the Hermit. The problems of the way

young people behave and the standards their elders
expect of them have always been a matter of debate.

What responsibility are we called to as parents, as
children, as children to our elderly parents . . . ?

Honour

The Hebrew word 'honour' means 'treat as weighty'.
It does not mean obey without question; it does not
simply mean be nice to them. There is something in
this command about our behaviour, our attitude and
our responsibility to our parents. It is a positive focus;
not a 'You are not to disobey your parents', but rather
the positive, 'Honour your father and mother'. The
training of children does not start with a series of neg-
atives, but with one positive.

How do we honour our parents?

According to the Anglican Catechism, this Commandment means, 'To love our parents, honour our
parents and succour our parents.' John Calvin wrote
that we should 'look up to those whom God has placed
over us and treat them with honour, obedience and
gratefulness'. The Oxford Thesaurus contains the following words for honour: 'reverence, respect, obedience, gratitude, trust, confidence, praise, attention,
esteem, adore, consideration and care'.

The honour that children must show to parents
cannot just be assumed as a right by parents. Mothers
and fathers must play their full roles in bringing up
their children. Too often, our society sells us the lie
that what is most important in life is where we get to,
what we can achieve in our job, how much money we

can earn, how much influence we can exert. These are not bad things in themselves, but when they become the driving force for life, it is at the expense of family life. So many busy fathers only ever see their children at weekends or on holidays.

Now it is not as easy as saying that no parents should have a job which expects that they have to work long hours and come home after their children have gone to bed. I am not saying that parents should always be at home by 5pm when their children return from school. But it is worth considering just how long we do spend with our children.

Mary Pytches, who has become a prolific author and speaker on the issue of family life, shoots down a common assumption that it is not the length of time you spend with a child, but the quality of time you spend. There is, she contends, no such thing as quality time which isn't also a decent quantity of time. And I believe she is right. The way to bring up a family, to gain their respect, love and obedience, is not to throw money at them, not to give them big presents regularly, not to take them on expensive holidays every year, but to show love to them in the relationship of parent to child.

A Member of Parliament I know has five children. He is also a practising barrister. He leads one of the busiest lives I know. It is often a struggle for him to make or find time to spend with his family. But he has set certain rules in place to carve out time for his family. He never stays away for the evening unless he is out of the country. He doesn't do early breakfast TV because he likes to have breakfast with his children. He tries to keep weekends as free as possible, and during the school holidays will regularly bring his children into the House of Commons to see where Daddy works, so they share a part of his life.

Being a parent is tough work. It requires us to love, care, nurture, teach and at times discipline our children. In 1968 the United Nations produced a Charter of Children's rights. The document details the rights that children should have, protecting them from exploitation. It is an excellent document, but it misses out any right for parents or guardians to discipline their children. We are told that God our Father disciplines us in the way that a human father disciplines his children, and far from showing that he doesn't care, it actually shows how much he loves the child, because he doesn't want to see the child hurt. Discipline is never for the reason of inflicting pain or shame; it is to teach the child a lesson so they will not harm themselves in the future.

The Bible seems to me quite clear on the responsibility of parents to discipline their children:

> Do not withhold your discipline from a child, if you punish them with a rod, they will not die.
>
> Proverbs 23:13 RSV

There does seem to be a set precedent that the loving thing for the parents to do in certain situations is to discipline their children. How this is done, I think, is up to each father, mother or guardian to work out for themselves. It must, however, be held alongside St Paul's advice to the fathers of Ephesus:

> Fathers, do not embitter your children, or they will become discouraged.
>
> Ephesians 6:4

Or as Martin Luther said, 'Spare the rod and spoil the child—that is true. But beside the rod keep an apple to give him when he has done well.' If parents are to expect obedience they must encourage that obedience.

The Bible also instructs parents to teach their children diligently, speaking of God and his ways, his law and his plans. Repeatedly it tells parents to tell their children the story of their origins. The family is where faith is handed on. It is not the duty of the minister or the Sunday school teacher to teach children about faith; it is the God-given duty of the parents.

> In the future when your son asks you, 'What is the meaning of the stipulations, decrees and laws the Lord our God has commanded us?' tell him . . .
>
> Deuteronomy 6:20–21

This is something my wife and I enjoy doing with our children. We have always prayed for them and with them and have set aside times to do that after breakfast and before they go to bed. We are the ones to whom God has entrusted our three boys and we must do everything we can to bring them up in the Christian faith.

This Commandment works best when the parent–child relationship is healthy. If our parents behave in a way which is compatible with that laid down for us in the Bible, it is easier for us to honour them. But whether we think they do deserve our honour or not this command does not say, 'Honour your father and mother if you think they are worth it!' although many of us would have found it easier if it did!

Gratitude and respect

I can say with all honesty that I do not find this easy. Disrespect is a great danger for me as my parents do not approve of many things I have done and do. For example, they did not approve of my marriage and did not attend our wedding. I know what it is like to have a very rough time at home. I have struggled with what this command means.

However, we should respect the experience that our parents have gained. We should also acknowledge the sacrifice that our parents have made. A child is frail during the first years of life, and parents make huge sacrifices in order to care physically and financially. As we grow up we can easily become removed from our parents; they don't seem to understand us and we certainly do not understand them. Mark Twain said:

When I was fourteen my father was so ignorant I could hardly bear him, but by the time I was twenty-one I was amazed to see how much he had learned in seven years.

Mark Twain's father had not changed, but Mark Twain had developed into a position where he could respect and honour his father. We should respect our parents because of all they have done to bring us into the world and raise us with the best they could possibly give. So before criticising them for what we think their shortcomings are, we need to realise how much we owe to them.

We can honour our parents by being open with them; it is one of the things that they really appreciate. Do they know about our friends and ambitions? So often I hear the refrain, 'But they just wouldn't understand.' But we have never even tried explaining, asking for their advice and wisdom. And so suspicion and mistrust can be created because of our lack of openness.

The book of Judges records the story of Samson, who can hardly be described as a mummy's boy! He used to love telling riddles, and when some people asked him of the meaning of one of them, he said, 'I haven't even explained it to my father and mother, so why should I explain it to you?' (Judges 14:16). He suggests that his parents were the first people in whom he confided. Next time you are in a quandary not knowing what to do, or you have something on your mind, could your parents be consulted? (You don't have to take their advice!)

We can also honour our parents by showing them warmth and affection. We all know how embarrassing it can be to be kissed by your mum outside the school gate with all your mates watching when you are ten. But we must resist the temptation to lose all physical contact with our parents. When there is no affection shown physically, the relationship can grow cold. There should be a time for telling each other, children and parents, that we love each other. The benefits of hugging our children can far outweigh the embarrassment.

Some young men I know who were sent away to

prep school at the age of seven, and then away to public school have never known their fathers as anything other than figures like army generals. They have never relaxed with their fathers, or been shown affection. The relationship has been characterised by an unemotional, stiff upper lip approach and, although it may look and feel very manly, it leaves deep wounds beneath the surface. These wounds affect them as they look for affection since they have never really learned how to give it or receive it in the context of their family.

Now the difficulty is that parents can sometimes become too possessive and not allow a growing freedom to their teenagers. As we said before we all know it is perfectly natural for a young bird to fly the nest when its time of nurture and care under its parents' wings is over. It wouldn't look too good if all these little nests were full of huge birds who refused to fly! In the same way, children reach the stage where it is only natural for them to assert their independence. They might do this through the music that they listen to, they might do it through the clothes that they wear. They might do it in all sorts of ways.

Now I am not saying that they should just be left to do whatever they want—that doesn't seem to me to be a particularly responsible approach—but parents must be supportive; let go and ease up at the same time. In the teen years young people start going out with one another, they start to find image and style, they start to have aspirations, they start to come into contact with alcohol and even some of the things we would want to keep them from at all cost. We cannot live their lives for them. Yes, they may make mistakes and when they do, wouldn't it be great if it were their parents whom they first turned to? We can give them advice, share our experiences of the things in our youth we did right and wrong, what we learned and how. To be there for them and to love them in the way we best can. I can remember a few years ago hearing the story of a father, telling his son that he either got his shoulder-length hair cut or he left home. The boy left home, and the father has never really been able to forgive himself. Loving does not mean possessing or even compelling the person to do whatever we want them to do. In Jesus' parable of the prodigal son, the father acts in such an unusual way that he grants the request of the son and gives him the land, his own land, to sell and lets him go. This is the way in which God has loved us. We must model his love in our families. It's a love which always desires the best, which always hopes and always protects, but also a love which doesn't possess, but frees.

Esteem and consideration

This is particularly relevant when we leave home to become students or leave home for work. We need to show consideration to our parents, to think carefully about them, to esteem them, to have great respect and high regard for them.

This may mean something as simple as not bad-mouthing them in public. To stand against the vast tide of opinion that assumes it is 'natural' to hate your in-laws, 'immature' to ask your parents' advice after you have left home, 'abnormal' to value the companionship of anyone much older than yourself. Let's not speak or act in a way which betrays a lack of respect.

We can show consideration and esteem by visiting them regularly. If we are hardly ever in contact with them, by letter, phone or through visits, it's not actually involving them in our lives.

Esteem and consideration also includes respecting their advice. The book of Proverbs encourages us: 'Listen my son to your father's instruction . . . do not forsake your mother's teaching' (Proverbs 4:1, 6:20). We can think we know best and that the older generation doesn't have a clue, that our parents do not have anything worthwhile to say. But they know us, their influence has helped to make us the people that we are, they have a longer experience of life and they have learned a lesson or two from the 'school of hard knocks'!

Does this command require total obedience?

While this command does require co-operation, it is not a *carte blanche* to all children to succumb to all the wishes, quirks and orders of their parents. We can see this in the way that Jesus worked with his family. There is a point in the gospel stories when he has been preaching near to his home town. Mark, the writer of the account, tells us that some of the older and more religious members of the community were accusing him of being mad, of losing his senses. Then we are told that his mother, his brothers and sisters came to the place where he was speaking in order to take him back to their home. 'When his family heard it, they went out to restrain him, for people were saying, "He has gone out of his mind"' (Mark 3:21 NRSV). It seems that Jesus' own family didn't understand him and wanted to take him away with them. Perhaps they were embarrassed by him, worried about what might happen to him or they may actually have believed with the other people that he had gone out of his mind. So they waited outside the crowded house where Jesus was teaching and healing and sent in for him. It's worth quoting the verses in full:

A crowd was sitting around him and they said to him, 'Your mother and brothers and sisters are outside, asking for you.' And he replied, 'Who are my mother and my brothers?' And looking at those who sat around him, he said, 'Here are my mother and brothers! Whoever does the will of God is my brother and sister and mother.'

Mark 3:31–35 NRSV

Jesus did not have an easy time with his family. Many commentators think that although his mother is often listed among the women who followed him in his three years of ministry, the rest of his family didn't. Jesus did not have a particularly easy family life; he was misunderstood; he was not supported as much as he could have been; he had a rough time of it.

But he still honoured them. One of the last things he did when he was dying, hanging from the cross, was to give one of his best friends responsibility to look after his mother. He is hanging there in complete agony, dying the cruellest and most painful death ever devised, and he thinks of his mother. He wants to be sure that she is provided for; he deeply loves and honours his mother and wants to make sure she will be comforted and looked after by his best friend when he is not around.

But what should we do when our parents advise us, or tell us to do something which we feel is in contradiction to our faith, or instruct us that we can't do a certain activity? Now there is obviously no complete blueprint, but if you are instructed, as a friend of mine was by her mother, to go and consult a medium to try and gain contact with her dead father, it seems quite proper to refuse, as this is clearly against the teaching of the Bible.

Our first allegiance is to God; we must honour him above everything else, and the Bible tells us that those who honour God, he himself will honour.

Remember the Sabbath day by keeping it holy. Six days you shall labour and do all your work, but the seventh day is a Sabbath to the Lord your God. On it you shall not do any work, neither you, nor your son or daughter, nor your manservant or maidservant, nor your animals, nor the alien within your gates. For in six days the Lord made the heavens and the earth, the sea, and all that is in them, but he rested on the seventh day. Therefore the Lord blessed the Sabbath day and made it holy.
Exodus 20:8–11

We may have got so many irons in the fire that we are in danger of putting the fire out. We may burn the candle at both ends and then realise we are not so bright after all. We live in a rat race and even if we win the race we will still be a rat and in fact we never seem to get out of the maze. Often we seem to be chasing two rabbits at the same time! If we don't live by priorities we will live by pressures.

Life at the end of the twentieth century seems to be lived at full pelt. In today's society the world rushes along at a fast rate, and we have to keep up or be trampled underfoot. Work is busy and efficiency and productivity are the names of the game. All the time we seek to advance, to produce more, to move forward, to do better than our previous generation, to increase productivity on last year, to become more efficient.

Advances in technology have made ours a highly sophisticated and organised society. We can pick up the phone and talk to relatives or business associates on the other side of the globe. We can get on a plane and go virtually anywhere in the world within a day, whereas for our great-grandparents the same distance would have taken them over six months. Communication is instant and increasingly available.

All of these things make our increasingly busy lives more and more hectic and frantic. More people last year took time off work for stress-related illnesses than ever before. Pressure to achieve more and more is all around; to be bigger and better and faster and stronger and richer. It is wise to stop and think about how living in such a driven society has affected us, our families and those around us.

I use the term 'driven' because I think it well sums up our modern society. We feel driven to achieve and succeed. This in turn leads us to working harder and longer. And outside of work it can lead to strained relationships in our private lives. The instant nature of our society, our food, our entertainment, our communications, and also our travel enters the personal world of relationships. We expect our relationships to be instantly right or workable and we cannot cope when we are called to work patiently at them, hence such high levels of breakdown in relationships.

Now, there's nothing wrong with activity, but when we see society around us disintegrate at the rate it is doing, it is important to ask the question, why is this happening? And one of the main reasons we see such disintegration is because of the lack of regard for this fourth command.

That may surprise you, because if I asked you which one of the Ten Commandments was least applicable today, you might point to this one. But which commandment do you think has the greatest effect on the health of the nation, upon family life and medical health? I would suggest that it is this fourth command. It is almost a health warning for us, not just a piece of good advice which belongs to a bygone age before the industrial or technological revolution, but an institution which we have ignored and continue to ignore at our peril.

To understand it we must briefly look at the first word of the command, because it does not begin with a negative, 'You shall not . . .', but with a 'Remember . . .'. You see, we were created to need a day of rest. Why? The reason is all part of our being made in the image of God. The first chapter of the Bible tells us that human beings were formed last in the created order, and given honour and distinction which none of the other creatures had: we were made in the image of God. And then the story goes on to say that on the seventh day 'God rested' after he had finished all the work of creating the heavens and earth. We may think that as humans we were the pinnacle, the climax of God's creation, but I don't think that is right. The climax is God resting from his work in creation and enjoying what he has made in fellowship and communion on the seventh day. In the same way that humans are following the Creator in the action of work, or in the desire to work, so we are told to remember the day of rest. We are made in the image of God, and as he rested, so must we. It's a pretty stunning thought, isn't it, that God took a rest? In the Bible we read '. . . in six days the Lord made the heavens and earth and on the seventh day he rested and was refreshed' (Exodus 31:17 RSV). The original language literally meant, 'He abstained from work and got his breath back!' So we are told to remember, to call to mind why we need time off. If God took a break it seems pretty logical that we need to, unless, that is, we think we are stronger than God . . .

This Commandment affirms that work is good. It is a desirable thing for men and women to spend time engaged in fulfilling work. Resting on the seventh day is dependent on the six working days. Now work is not simply limited to what we are paid for. There is a distinction between work and employment. But we all have a desire to do things, to make a difference, to be able to contribute to society, to play our part. Part of the tragedy of unemployment which is so often missed—if it is viewed simply as a financial problem— is that the in-built God-given desire to work is lying fallow and frustrated in a human being who has so much unfulfilled potential in them. That is one of the reasons why we should support policies that will enable many long-term unemployed people to get back to work. But the main purpose of this command isn't to talk about work, but the one day in seven when we don't work. It is a constant reminder to follow God, and to obey his instructions for enjoying his goodness. However, because we are all living with the consequences of what is called 'the Fall', which describes the broken relationship between humans and God caused by our disobedience and our turning away from him and his ways, many things which are in themselves positive are just considered as negative and inhibiting. We must not fall into the trap of limiting this command to a list of things which God prohibits on a Sabbath. By the time of Jesus the experts in the Jewish law had turned the Fourth Commandment into a travesty of what was intended. Because there were thirty-nine letters in the Hebrew sentence of this command, they had broken the Commandment down into the thirty-nine main areas of work and then divided each section into another thirty-nine parts, making a huge 1,521 'Thou shalt nots' out of this one command.

In England we are always being told horror stories about the so-called Victorian Sunday, which was devoted to painful inaction. Children were confined to playing with their toys and being kept out of sight, and everyone else had to dress up, have as little fun as possible and spend the whole day in religious boredom. But before we have too much of a go at them, let's stop and think. What might they have got right? I'd suggest what they got right was the change.

There is a great danger that we accept things in our materialistic world simply because we have always known them to be like that. However, through this Commandment God asks us to question our ways of going about things. He asks us to take a long, hard look at the way in which he has made us, and to look at our predecessors and try and learn how he really does intend us to live.

I remember hearing a story some time ago of a Communist country where the seven-day week was scrapped and in its place was put a ten-day week, with just one rest day every ten days. The aim was to try and produce more, to be more effective and efficient. However, the breaking of the normal pattern of six days' work and one day off decreased productivity and so the idea was scrapped.

This serves as an example of why we need a day off; it is not to make us less effective or lazy, but to make us more effective. The person who had one of the most significant roles in the invention of the modern motor car said something very interesting about a day of rest. Henry Ford, who set up the Ford Motor Company said that it is not only good religion but also good business not to work for seven days without a day of rest. He said that his company would have had the famous Model-A car in production six months earlier had he forbidden his engineers to work on Sundays. Fatigue set in during the frantic effort to meet production deadlines. 'It took us all week to straighten out the mistakes that we made on the day we should have rested!'

We need to rest one day in seven, to do something different from our normal routine, to spend time with our family and those we are closest to, to take time out from the business of everyday working life. Now it is obvious that nowadays not everyone can take the same day off. If they did the whole country would shut down. We are hugely in the debt of the emergency services, the public transport system and those who work in the public services. Many cannot take Sunday off.

But let us first look at the responsibility of those who can.

It is a good thing that there is still a widely respected day off for the majority of the country. As this country is built on Christian principles it has traditionally been a Sunday, and there doesn't seem to be any need to change that. Now the smart ones among us will be quick to point out that the Sabbath referred to in the Old Testament is not the same as our Sunday. And that's true. Orthodox Jews still celebrate their day of rest on the Sabbath—our Saturday. But for the early Christians it was not enough for them simply to celebrate the Jewish calendar. Because Jesus Christ had risen from the dead on the first day of the week, the Sunday, they wanted to celebrate this life-changing fact. So for the Christian church Sunday became quite quickly the regular day of worship for the whole community. They would meet very early in the morning or in the evening and listen to the apostles' teaching, have fellowship and prayer and share in bread and wine. In the ensuing years this became the regular pattern in the church. So much so that by the time of the Emperor Constantine, Christianity became the formal religion of the state, and Sunday the day of rest for the whole country.

So we are still today living within a society which has traditionally regarded Sunday as the national day of rest for most people. Now this has been a good thing because this has meant that on one day in the week there is the possibility of spending good time with family and friends, of taking a break from the pressures of life, and relaxing, recuperating, building up those energy levels and building up relationships which can too easily dwindle if we take no quality time in each other's presence. Sunday is important as a family day.

Now forgive me, if you live alone, if I just talk for a moment to those who have families. One of the saddest things about our society is the disintegration of the traditional family unit. I don't want to go into any indepth analysis here, but simply to raise the issue that one of the reasons this has happened is because we have not spent time with each other. Sunday provides the best opportunity for a family to get together, to eat together, to go out together, to do activities together, because children aren't at school and Mum and Dad are less likely to be at work. We have been so short-sighted, most of the time, in allowing all kinds of pressures on time which we could have spent with family and friends.

The biggest example of this has to be the legislation regarding Sunday trading. Now there are many issues involved here: small shopkeepers being driven out of business as the larger stores take the majority of the money; shops being forced to open on a Sunday against their will simply to keep afloat. But one of the main worries has to be the fact that many people are being forced to work on a Sunday against their will. And in spite of Government protests this is already happening as those who are applying for jobs in retail are having to be prepared to work any hours asked. Many firms are drawing up contracts which stipulate that employees must be prepared to work on a Sunday. The upshot is that many who do not want to work on a Sunday are forced to do so. But some people do want to work and surely that's a good thing. Or is it? Why do they want to work? They want to work because they want the extra money. So people are being driven to work because of the financial gain. At what cost? The cost of their relationships between their family and friends. And who are the majority of those who work in retail part time? Working mums.

So on the very day when families have the possibility of being together, the mother is not there because she's working, whether voluntarily or involuntarily. It's been proved by many studies that Sunday trading doesn't mean that people spend more money. It just means that people spread their spending over seven days instead of six. On top of this is the extra traffic, pollution, noise and emergency services which need to be put on. Sunday trading may seem a pleasant choice at this time. We are told that it actually helps family life, as 'families enjoy going shopping together'. Well, I don't know about you, but the times I have seen families most fraught is when they are out shopping together! I fear that in a few years' time we will understand the effect of all this on our society and realise we made one of the most short-term, money-centred decisions ever, the consequences of which will haunt us for decades to come.

So should we shop on Sundays? My advice would be not, unless you really have to for things which cannot wait until Monday. By such an attitude we make a conscious break from the regular routine of life. I've no desire to draw up a point-by-point programme of what we should or shouldn't do on Sundays, but to suggest certain principles for the right way forward in the light of this command.

Because the need for balance in life between work and rest is a law written into every cell in our bodies, we need one day out of seven, twenty-four hours a week, 1,440 minutes or 86,000 seconds to rest. It amounts to seven weeks out of the year. Now that might seem too much, because time for us all is a precious commodity, but if we are to live a healthy and fulfilled life, we will need to take heed.

One doctor said, 'The periods of rest I prescribe to my patients are often Sabbaths in arrears.'

But for a minority in the country, our work demands that we work on Sundays. Doesn't that go against the whole sense of this Commandment? I said earlier that there are some who provide a vital service to the community on a Sunday: the medical profession, the emergency services and public services. It does seem important that we have one day in the week when the majority of the working nation can take a break. Obviously not everyone can or else the country would quickly grind to a halt. It's a bit hard, isn't it, that while we take the day off, these other people are left running things? Now when this Commandment was first given, the nation of Israel was called a theocracy, that is, the whole nation was based on God's command. There was no divide between religious and secular. God was in charge of everything; everyone was a worshipper. Now this is obviously not true today.

So for those who find themselves having to work on Sundays, I would say that they must find another day during the week to take a complete break from work, taking time off away from the normal routine. And this applies to ministers, like myself, for whom Sunday can be the busiest day of the week. Taking a day off in the week is not a luxury, it is part of the created order, and it is a command of God. Why? Because the God who made us knows best how we should work and he made us to rest one day in seven.

Sometimes it may be quite a struggle to take Sunday off. You may be asked to work regularly on Sunday and be in danger of losing your job if you don't. It may seem easier just to give in. Here are two instances where people took a hard choice about Sunday working and things worked out better for them.

Osborne House on the Isle of Wight was one of Queen Victoria's houses. When she first arrived on the island to take up residence it was a Saturday. All the local tradesmen wanted the business of the royal household and, on the Sunday, they sent their servants and foremen with their cards and said they hoped Her Majesty would appoint them as her suppliers. On the Monday morning, the Queen looked at the cards and said to her servant, 'Are the cards of all the local tradesmen here?' 'No, your majesty,' he replied. 'There is one card missing—from the large grocer in the village.' Queen Victoria asked why his card was not there. 'I contacted him,' the servant replied, 'but he said he wouldn't send his card on a Sunday.' Queen Victoria immediately said, 'That is the man I want to supply groceries for the royal household.'

In 1924 during the Olympic Games, a Christian athlete called Eric Liddell had a preliminary draw on a Sunday. He refused to run, raising doubts about his loyalty to his king and country. He was subsequently moved from the 100 metres race to the 400 metres. Just before he ran the race someone gave him a piece of paper with a Bible quote: 'Those who honour me I will honour' (1 Samuel 2:30). He ran. He won and broke the world record for the 400 metres. The story is graphically told in the film *Chariots of Fire*.

Today we live in a restless world. Life is full of unfinished tasks. The temptation is to cram everything into every single minute of every single hour every single day. The Creator himself made us to work and that is good, but he also made us to take time out. We need to look closely at our life and the lives of those around us. We need to remember this is not just a nice suggestion for those who like things like this. It's one of the Maker's instructions!

You shall not misuse the name of the Lord your God,
for the Lord will not hold anyone guiltless who
misuses his name.
Exodus 20:7

It is always fascinating to see surveys of the most popular names for the year and how fashions and trends change and develop. Some of the most popular names now were very uncommon thirty years ago. Nowadays we tend to choose names because we like the sound of them, rather than for what they mean. But each of our names means something and that's not only true of our first names, it is also true of our surnames. It does not take much to work out what profession families with the name Blacksmith originally came from, nor should we be surprised that the surname Smith is the most common considering there were so many who worked as smiths. Some people spend time and effort researching what the origins of their name are. Why? Because they attach a certain amount of importance to what their name means, what the origins of it are. It is something very personal to them.

Controversy in the courts often involves libel or slander cases, or cases coming back before the courts with doubts over the surety of the conviction. In such cases the people involved talked of their joy at having 'their name cleared'. Previously, when anyone had mentioned their name, everyone had associated them with being criminals, but now their names have been cleared and they are no longer considered the guilty parties.

In recent years libel cases have been very much in the news as those in public life take a newspaper or magazine to court over statements printed which are deemed to damage their reputation, soil their name or bring them down. Often such cases have been hotly contested and some have led to national newspapers forking out hundreds of thousands of pounds because they have been found guilty of publishing damaging statements or stories about a person which are unfounded and therefore bring that person into disrepute.

We too have the same desire to keep our name respected. If there are malicious stories or unfair criticisms going around about us we do not like it and we feel very offended.

But how would you feel if every time someone hurt themselves, or something went wrong in their lives, or just generally in an offensive manner, they used your name, 'Oh, J.John', to show their displeasure? Well, I don't know about you, but I think I'd be a little offended and then get angry. Because none of us would want our name being used like mud.

And the same is true of God.

But there's even more to the background of this

command. In the Old Testament, a person's soul and their name were almost indistinguishable. A person's whole personality was present in their name. Therefore to know a person's name was to gain an insight into their nature and in some way acquire a relationship with them. There is a story in the Bible about Jacob wrestling with a stranger and neither is winning, and Jacob asks the stranger for his name, but the stranger won't give it to him, because it would give him an advantage. Names are important. The whole Bible is a story of people who have names which have meanings; some change their name, because the original name no longer fits. For example, once Abram is told by God that he is going to be the father of many nations, his name is changed from Abram, which means 'exalted father', to Abraham, which means 'father of many'. When his son Isaac marries and his wife Rachel has twins, the first one who comes out is hairy and the second one is holding the heel of his brother. So the first one is given the name Esau which means 'hairy' and the second son is given the name Jacob, which means 'he grasps the heel'.

The name of God

Moses, who led the Israelites out of slavery in Egypt, not only received the Ten Commandments, but was also the first one to whom God reveals his name. Up till that time God was just called by his attributes, e.g. 'God Almighty' or 'God the Provider'. His true name was not known. Moses saw a bush in flames but not burning. Realising this was not an everyday occurrence he braced himself for something special and then and there he was called to be the one who would lead the people out of slavery in Egypt into the Promised Land. But he insisted that if he was going to do this, to represent God in front of Pharaoh, the ruler of Egypt, and say that God had sent him, he must know God's name. God tells Moses that his name is 'I am' or 'I am who I am'. That is, God's name is the one who exists, who always was, who is and who is to come. And we are told that this name is powerful. For if this name is called upon now, his name, his presence and his will are invoked. God hasn't revealed himself by an image, or as a concept, or by a riddle, but with a name. And that name is part of his self-revelation. Inviting us to be on first-name terms with him, the living God has made himself vulnerable and open to abuse.

From that time on the name of God has been treated with the highest regard by the Jewish people. They use his name very rarely in speech or even in worship, and actually use a different word in worship and public speech to avoid having to use the name. The phrase, 'The Name of the Lord' appears more than 750 times in the Old Testament. His name was so highly regarded that if a scribe was copying a manuscript and reached the four consonants, YHWH, which stood for the Lord, he had to observe strict regulations: to wash, to put on new clothes, to use a new quill, and once he had started writing it he could not stop after two letters if one of his friends walked in. God's name was held in the highest regard. And the reason was because of this Commandment.

So, for the Jewish people this command meant that the name of God was to be treated with awe and respect.

But what does it mean for us now?

Swearing

Well, the most obvious application of this is not to use the name of the Lord in swearing. I think we have become numb to the shocking fact of just how often and how indiscriminately God's name is taken in vain. God's name is used as a swear word in the playground, on the bus, in magazines, on the TV, in shops, at work. Everywhere we go people take the name of God in vain. The other day I watched a video with some young people. The certificate that had been put on the film was PG—no age limit, but young children should watch the film with their parents' permission or guidance. From the very first scene the names Jesus and God were used in every scene as swear words. Yet this was obviously not thought by those who gave the film its PG certificate to be offensive enough to fit the description of 'bad or offensive language' which might give the film a higher certificate. We may well be forgiven for asking the question, 'Is there nothing sacred?'

My wife's name is Killy—it is very precious to me. Killy is the name of someone I love very much. If people used my wife's name casually or flippantly it would concern me. In just the same way, it should concern us when God's name is used by people in a callous way. If we treat his name as nothing, this

Commandment teaches us that 'God will not hold anyone guiltless' when we do so.

We should not use the name of God flippantly. This includes saying, for example, 'I swear by God I will do it' for just a trivial matter. Jesus had something to say about this in Matthew 5:33–37. When we give someone a pledge we should not swear by anything, but let our 'yes' mean yes and our 'no' mean no. It sounds so simple, doesn't it? But we are so bad at keeping our word. What a difference it would make to us and to those around us if we all began just saying very simply yes or no and that was enough; we had given our word. To say what we mean and mean what we say!

Vows

But what about using God's name in a court of law or in a marriage ceremony? Well a marriage ceremony is treated by the church as a covenant between the two people and God, a vow made not only in the sight of God but with God. Therefore it seems good for that to be acknowledged in the vows that are made. As for court, although the Quakers refuse to swear on the Bible, it should not cause a problem for us. There are two reasons why. There is a story of a judge who had a young boy in front of him giving witness against an older man. Both sides were claiming different stories and each was adamant that their story was true. A lot depended on the testimony of the young boy.

'What is your favourite subject at school?' the judge asked him as he stepped into the witness box.

'Geography, sir,' replied the boy.

'What do you do in geography?'

'Draw maps, sir.'

'Have you drawn any interesting maps recently?'

'Yes, sir, a map of Canterbury.'

The judged looked pleased.

'Have you ever been to Canterbury?'

The boy nodded.

'Did you see the cathedral?'

'Yes, sir.'

'Whose house is it?' asked the judge, anticipating the answer God.

'The Archbishop of Canterbury's house, sir.'

'But who do people worship when they go into the cathedral?'

'God, sir.'

'Don't you think that God must be very big and important for people to worship him in such a grand cathedral?'

'Yes, sir.'

'In a moment I'm going to ask you to promise to tell the truth by swearing in the name of God whom people worship when they go into the cathedral. It's going to be very important then that you tell the whole truth.'

In his name

We read in the New Testament that Jesus' followers did miracles and healings 'in the name of Jesus'. His name was powerful and when they pronounced healing in his name people were healed. It was not their own healing power that they relied upon, but the healing power of Jesus. That's why they did things in his name. The prophets in the Old Testament speak in the name of the Lord. And what they speak comes true. There are also people who claim they are speaking in God's name but they are actually just promoting their own ideas or their own plans. To those people who use God's name as backing for what is not of God, who put the words, 'The Lord says . . .' before something which is really just, 'I say . . .' there is a severe warning. God's name should not be manipulated or swung behind a cause to justify it.

This means that we should be careful not to use God's name to promote ourselves. Cult leaders often allure people to follow them and give them all their money, their possessions and their lives by claiming to have a special message for the world from God. And recently we have just seen another disaster as over fifty people took their own lives because of the power of the cult leader who claimed that what he was saying was from God. Orthodox mainstream Christianity has stated and affirmed all down the centuries that God's word is the Bible and anyone who comes claiming to have a new message, which is not in line with the Bible, is not telling the truth and God's judgement will be on them.

We need to be aware of those who ask us to give our support to a political party because they say they are God's choice. There have been times in history when parties have claimed to stand for God and it's obvious they did not! We only have to look back at Hitler's Third Reich to see that. He invoked God's name and said he was doing God's will, and it has long been a source of shame that the church did not stand up to him sufficiently. In America we see how politicians try to get church leaders and denominations to endorse their political agendas.

In our country there are Christians in all three main political parties. A friend of mine who worked for a Christian MP said that whenever the MP was asked to talk about his faith he would do so on a personal level, and would never say that all Christians should vote for his party. In fact he would never accept invitations which asked him to speak about why his Christian faith had led him to the political party he represented, precisely because he did not want to disobey this command of taking God's name in vain, invoking God's name for his own ends.

Tony Blair, the leader of the Labour Party and a professing Christian, said in an interview in October 1994, 'One of the things I can't stand is when we start going on about God, because it's usually for reasons which have very little to do with religion' (*The Observer* 2 October). In other words, people in public life talk about God to try and swing their own political agenda. To those in public life this command would forbid the name-dropping of God to further their own career or their cause. To those of us who hear so many claims and counter claims, we must be wise and not taken in by what might be a cynical attempt to gain popularity. God is not the justification for anyone's agenda.

There is a true story about one of the most influential theologians of this century, Karl Barth, who as a young man, was brought up in the liberal, rational atmosphere of enlightened Germany. He was a typical intellectual theologian who believed very little of the Bible and had reasoned most things away. At the outbreak of the First World War all his lecturers and the theologians who had taught him most, signed a public letter declaring their support for the aims of Kaiser Wilhelm. This was the action that made Karl Barth stop and think. Suddenly everything that he had held dear lay in tatters, as the people he so respected had given themselves to a quite unjustifiable cause. He saw their belief for what it was and went back to the Bible to think it all out again. He came to completely different conclusions!

The power of the name of God

This command also forbids the use of the name of God for magical purposes. It seems wise therefore to say something about things spiritual. The Bible never denies that there are all sorts of powers that are at work in the world. It is not simply God who is at work. And power has dangers. Pylons stretching across the countryside carry high voltage electric cables. The same atomic power that lights a city and fuels its industries can annihilate a city if it gets out of control. Chernobyl was a nightmare. The power under the bonnet of a car can kill and maim. And regarding political power, we must remember that Hitler rose to power through democratic means. Power can always be wrongly used.

Spiritual power is no exception to the rule. I quote

from Dr John White, psychologist and writer, in his book *When the Spirit Comes in Power* (Hodder & Stoughton):

> People who have never experienced the raw impact of spiritual power find it hard to imagine that it could be dangerous.

Dr White goes on to tell how, although all power is originally traceable back to God, not all power is used correctly.

In this command, God makes it very clear that his name is not to be used in magic; this might mean curses and the like. I think the sense of this command also involves all magic that is an invocation of another power. Nowhere in the Bible does it say that the only power in the universe is God. On the contrary, Scripture is quite clear that there are all sorts of powers and principalities around which humans tap into. Tampering with them is like playing with fire; it's dangerous and we are handling something much bigger than we can control. Practices like seances, ouija boards, tarot card reading, spiritualist meetings, astrological charts, horoscopes, palmistry, and so on should be avoided and opposed because they are playing with the dark powers of the universe, invoking that which is not good. The Bible says that the power behind all opposition to God is the 'father of all lies'. These practices leave the individual or group wide open and vulnerable to the influence of the dark powers which are called evil. Interest in such things is growing constantly. In 1993 the third best-selling paperback was a book of horoscopes. More and more people are tampering with the occult and becoming fascinated and drawn into that spiritual world. If you are tempted to get involved in such things, I urge you to keep clear. Time after time, week after week, I hear sad stories about those who have become involved in the occult out of simple curiosity or a desire to tap into some power. And without exception I hear of their lives becoming one long nightmare as they try to extricate themselves from it, realising too late that what they thought they had control over has now got control over them; that something far bigger than themselves has got its claws into them.

If this command forbids us to use God's name wrongly and for magic, and he is the all-loving good God, then how much more dangerous it is to invoke the name of beings who are dark and sinister, and to get involved with things we really have no idea about.

One of the things this command teaches us is that, contrary to the way modern culture views words, they are not like price labels which we can attach to things and make them mean anything we want to. Words have points of reference, they are important. We cannot just bandy them around as if they are really of no value. That means being careful with the words we use, not overplaying or underplaying things, letting our yes be yes and our no, no. In regards to God this may mean certain changes. For example try and cut out all references to God which aren't reverential and respectful. Because in so doing we are acknowledging that when we talk about God we are not talking about an invention of our own, or imagination or even faith, or some being that we can box and keep. We are talking about the living, holy, powerful God whose name should not be messed with or used and abused or taken for granted, but rather should be treated with awe and respect.

> *You shall not make for yourself an idol in the form of anything in heaven above or on the earth beneath or in the waters below. You shall not bow down to them or worship them; for I, the Lord your God, am a jealous God, punishing the children for the sin of the fathers to the third and fourth generation of those who hate me, but showing love to a thousand generations who love me and keep my commandments.*
>
> Exodus 20:4–6

We have come to one of the commandments some people think is most irrelevant to us today. After all, who today would seriously believe that God was a little statue or picture? Who today would worship something false? We think we are far too sophisticated to be caught worshipping something that is false.

The problem today isn't that we don't worship God. Many do not even believe in God, or at least a God that would demand anything from us. As products of the twentieth century we are inheritors of a way of thinking called the Enlightenment, which simply means that unless we can see it and prove it, then it cannot exist; God is so far outside my experience and understanding, he can never really be known. In this world many have dispensed with the idea of God. In previous centuries the idea of God was important, because it has helped to explain things like science and creation. Belief in God helped to regulate how people behaved because they had been told that that's what God wanted. But now we say we have come of age. We don't need God. We have scientists who have explained the universe for us, we have laws and democracy which tell us how we should act towards one another and we are fortunate enough to be able to stand on our own two feet. What we need is to learn to be fully human, to be ourselves. People used to think they needed God to help them do that; now we don't!

The founding editor of one of the largest women's magazines said, 'By the year 2000 I hope we will raise our children without any reference to God.'

So is this Commandment relevant to us in these remaining years of the twentieth century? Who is going to waste their time creating an idol who they know can do nothing for them? There have always been a few extreme groups who have believed in strange mystic powers of some god, but that really isn't a problem most of us have. I mean, when was the last time you went into a person's house and they had an altar to a god, or a statue on the mantelpiece which they claimed to be a god? No, this Commandment was perhaps necessary for those primitive people who used to worship trees and little carved images, and the like, but they didn't know any better. We do. What danger have we of making an idol and calling it God?

We can see how modern western thinking has convinced itself that this is a command which can just be disregarded. It was needed in times when people were prone to such delusions, but not in our culture. Well, that may have been true a number of years ago, but things have changed. Human reason isn't after all the unchallenged point of departure for all knowing. Yes, we have seen tremendous progress and modernisation, great developments and leaps forward in technology, but we still remain battered by problems of our humanness. We have stressed the individual as the free person, but have realised that it's not actually true, nor is it the way forward. We see increased alienation and the fracturing of society. There is a sense of crisis. Problems with the environment, world poverty, political change and instability, the breakdown of community, HIV and AIDS—the list is endless. But what it has led to for many people is a real spiritual search, realising that this cannot be it, that everything isn't right, that there must be something more. And so we see the shelves of our bookshops filled with books on self-awareness and self-fulfilment, on discovering the meaning of life. We are as a culture characterised by pick-and-mix—you choose what looks most attractive to you and work it into your scheme of things. There are no rules apart from just take anything you want to.

Someone said recently that today we treat life and the world like a smörgåsbord—one of those Swedish meals with every different kind of dish you could think of on it. And we all just cut off little bits and taste them and if we like it we cut off a bigger bit. We take as many different bits as possible to satisfy us. The more the merrier. The search is on to find the belief or object, the person or job, that can bring me the most fulfilment. Anything which doesn't add to my quality of life, my pleasure, my well-being or my fulfilment I will disregard. We only have to look at the breakdown in marriage and relationships in general to see the truth of this fact. We're on the hunt for the most fulfilling lifestyle.

This philosophy of life has led to a huge rise in interest in things 'spiritual', as people realise that material goods don't bring them the happiness they had expected. So from being a dirty word, 'spiritual' has become a buzz word as people try and fill the gaping hole which isn't met by the immediate world. So we see all around us many, especially young people, who dabble in all sorts of spirituality, especially meditative types which link themselves into worlds beyond or experiences outside themselves or self-awareness of their spiritual inner resources or those of mother earth. Now much could be said on this subject, but I want to concentrate on just one area because I think it is one of the most alluring.

God and the natural world

It seems strange to think it is only a few years ago that we were made aware of the reality of our ecological crisis, an imminent danger, a huge question mark over our future as humans and the future of our planet. This has led us all to becoming more conscious of the way we steward the resources of the earth and our responsibilities to the non-human creation. This has no doubt been a very good thing. However, it has led some groups to put such emphasis on the importance and sanctity of planet earth that it has led to the creation being viewed as the god who is present in everything, tangible and capable of being tapped into, and visible in the trees and flowers, all animals and elements. Part of this has been a reaction against God 'out there', a transcendent being who has nothing to do with this world, totally and utterly removed. And so we say God is located in the midst of us, tangible in that tree, that flower, that sunset. There has been a growing interest in things like crystals and rituals which take us back to the earth. This has so caught hold of some 'green' environmental groups that it has led them to what is called pantheism—thinking which locates God in everything around us; God is that plant, that tree, and so on. This is one of the things that this Commandment warns us against. God is not located in creation. Nothing can contain him. He is not that tree or flower, that sunset or that moonbeam. God is not localised in created matter.

You may be able to think of groups and people you know who have fallen into this trap. There is no way, you say, that you would ever think of worshipping a flower! But let's go back to the idea I shared earlier that we are living in a society dominated by a 'pick-and-mix' mentality. You might not hug trees or plunge your hands into the ground to become 'one with nature', because it's not quite your style. But I would suggest that the reason most people don't do this is because it doesn't work for them. If it did work, they would do it. We search around for things that will 'work' for us. We wander through the supermarket of life and take from the shelves anything that we think might give us fulfilment and may add to our quality of life. The phrase 'if it works for you . . .' is the slogan which sums up our attitude to life and what we can get from it. If it feels right, we will do it; if we can get some strength out of it, we might as well; if it works for us why shouldn't we do it, use it, buy into it . . . worship it?

What is idolatry?

We may not have little statues of gods and goddesses around our homes, but we may have found something which absorbs and focuses our lives so that, in effect, we have bowed down to it. Not physically, but in a way that makes something our *raison d'être*, our reason to be. If we just look around we can see things which people live for: relationships, jobs, that promotion, the larger house, a more powerful car, more fame, more prestige, that music system, those deep desires which show what really is the most important thing in our lives. And that is the place where God should be, the most important, most all-consuming passion. And anything that is there instead of him is an idol.

Idolatry is misdirected worship. Worship isn't just singing. It's the thing we live our lives for, it is an attitude of mind and heart. We've all heard of car enthusiasts who have been described as 'worshipping their cars'. The Bible makes it clear that anything that takes number one place in our lives is our 'god' and if that isn't the true and living God, what we have is a false idol. In his book, *God's Good Life* (IVP 1972), Dr David Field says that an idol is 'anything which detracts from the heartfelt devotion that properly belongs to

God'. That is a good definition. God is the one who deserves all our devotion simply because he is God.

What shape is our idol? What are we living for? What is our heart's ultimate desire? What is our driving principle, our *raison d'être*? Your answer to these questions will show what you are worshipping, what you are truly serving.

There are three areas the Bible points to where we humans are susceptible to slipping into idolatry, and these are the areas of money, sex and satisfaction.

Jesus says quite clearly that as far as money is concerned humanity has a clear choice:

> No-one can serve two masters. Either he will hate the one and love the other or he will be devoted to the one and despise the other. You cannot serve both God and Money.
>
> Matthew 6:24

In fact, the word Jesus used for money was 'mammon', a word which covered money and wealth. In the first century if you lived to acquire more and more wealth you were serving a god. Jesus points out that we cannot serve two masters. If we live for wealth we cannot live all out for God. Now worshipping wealth isn't restricted to those who are pursuing million-pound business deals, or who are close to reaching their first, second or third million. No, this is a danger you and I also face. It has to do with our attitude and what is our number one priority. The subject of wealth is something which Jesus talked about with great seriousness. In the gospels it is his second most important topic of teaching and conversation, only capped by the amount of time he talks about the kingdom of God. He warned people against the dangers of worshipping wealth.

One of the saddest stories in the New Testament is that of the rich man who comes to Jesus and asks what he must do to have eternal life. After a brief ground-setting exercise, Jesus tells the rich man that he must sell everything he has, give the money to the poor and follow him. Now some have taken this as a command to all Christians and have advocated poverty for all who would follow Christ. That is not doing justice to the context in which Jesus first spoke this. Jesus says these words because the man worshipped mammon; he worshipped wealth. That was the thing he had to give up to receive eternal life, because until he did, he could not follow Jesus. There was this huge anchor of love of wealth holding him back. Jesus had already said that it wasn't possible to serve two masters. He met someone who thought he could and so he threw the gauntlet down and the Bible says the man went away heavy-hearted because he had great wealth (Luke 18:18–25). He could not give up his false idol to follow and worship the living God.

The love of money

The Bible says that the love of money is the root of all kinds of evil. It is a fact that other gods like that of wealth actually do not do us any good at all. Even Madonna realises this:

> The more money you have, the more problems you have. I went from making no money to making comparatively

a lot and all I've had is problems. Life was much simpler when I had no money . . .

A book in the Old Testament points out that the person who loves money can never get enough of it, and that was written over 3,000 years ago. Some things don't change. But what about us? Do wealth and material possessions hold a driving fascination? Are they our goal? Because if they are, we need to be aware that not only are they set up against God, but they will ruin our lives and will not deliver what they promise. Look at what some immensely rich people have said on the subject:

> I never took pleasure in earning money. Money is not necessarily related to happiness. Maybe it is related to unhappiness.
>
> John Paul Getty

> My most fervent hope is that I'll meet a man who loves me for myself and not for my money.
>
> Christina Onassis

> It's fine to make money. It isn't fine to make money your god.
>
> Sinead O'Connor, singer

Two hundred years ago the biggest and most impressive buildings were churches and cathedrals, the places where people met to worship God. But drive through a town or city today and you will see that the buildings that are the biggest, the most expensive and architecturally sophisticated are not churches, but banks, financial companies and big shopping malls. Why? Because money is the modern day god and each generation will erect buildings which reflect their priorities. We see church after church with appeals to raise money for their renovation, but have you ever seen a bank with an appeal to renovate its premises?

Who do you worship?

Some people are in no serious danger of worshipping money. They are far too much a 'people person' to fall into that trap. Their life revolves around people and friendships, perhaps one in particular. Of course, relationships and friendships are important. In fact I'd go as far as to say that we only really know ourselves when we are in relationship with God and others. God made us to need others and also to be able to give. That is true of a community and also true of close intimate friendship. But we can slip into worshipping other people. For some people, their partner becomes the one around whom their life revolves. Everything they do is centred around them, everything they wear is what the other person wants them to wear, all their hope is invested in that one person.

Marriage of course is an exclusive, unconditional relationship but it is never right to afford to another human being the place that only God deserves; to put someone above God in our loyalties, in our time commitments, in our hope, with our future, is not right. I have seen relationship after relationship collapse because the people raised each other to the level of God, and when the other person could no longer fill that role, when the relationship shattered irrecoverably, they couldn't cope with it and had to withdraw in confusion and disappointment. The person they thought could meet all their needs could do no such thing.

For others, and especially those in their teens, the danger is that someone in the public eye becomes an idol. A pop star, a Gladiator, a film star, a supermodel or perhaps a rebel. Years ago I talked with a teenage girl about why she was a vegetarian and she gave me the startling reason, 'Well, a friend of mine asked me what Morrisey [at that time lead singer of a band called The Smiths] would think about me if he walked into the room and because he is a vegetarian I knew he wouldn't like me eating meat so I gave it up.' She went on to add, 'It's amazing, it's like he's everywhere, watching me and seeing everything I do.' Now I know this is perhaps an extreme example, but who are your idols? Who calls the shots in your life about what you wear, how you spend your money, who you mix with? Are you a slave to them? What shape is your false idol?

For others still their god, their false idol is pleasure—that is, their desires. This includes food, but it is not simply restricted to it. The Bible teaches clearly that all good things come from God, but they have their rightful place in his scheme of things. The trouble comes when people pursue pleasure as their number one aim in life. A couple of years ago Janet Jackson entitled her album *The Pleasure Principle* and it's a very fitting title for this decade. Today our country is full of hedonists. They may not know it; they may even be offended if they were called one, but a hedonist is someone whose idol is pleasure, whose god in life is enjoyment and personal satisfaction.

So we see people bowing down at any altar, to any idol that will give them pleasure, whether it's sex, music or food. But for some the biggest danger is not pleasure, but themselves.

Psychologist Stafford Clark was surely right when he said, 'No one is born prejudiced against other people, but everyone is prejudiced in favour of themselves.' The most common form of idolatry that goes on in this world today is of people worshipping themselves. The best example of this is the famous person who seems so infatuated with their own ego that everything around them focuses on them and the rest of the world has to take second place. John Lennon made that infamous declaration when as a member of The Beatles he said, 'We are more popular than Jesus.' We may believe in God, we may even believe we worship God and have no problem with idols, but think about it: in what ways do we set ourselves up as idols—in terms of the status we want, in terms of the recognition we require, in terms of the attention we must have?

God alone

Idols must go; they must be torn down, because only God is worthy of the position of God. Nothing else should challenge his authority, his position as head of our lives. Anything which sets itself up against God is playing the part of God, taking a place which is not rightfully theirs. It is an idol. We are warned against making idols because idols restrict our concept of God.

They push God off to the side, or perhaps off the stage altogether. Now lots of things might restrict someone's concept of God: it might be money, it might be friends, it might be pleasure, it might be belief in God-in-everything. Intensely religious people are prone to put God in a box and just get him out on Sundays. Or their view of God is too small. They've decided in their own minds what God can or cannot do. It might be that we have had a great view of God in the past, or that we have had a wonderfully moving experience of God, or that we can look back to a time when God did great things for us. And it's those times, or that experience or that situation which dominates our thinking about God today. Rather than letting God be God, we're content that we have him in our minds the way he was previously. So we remain static and don't grow in our relationship with him. We begin to dictate our terms and ask God to be what we want him to be.

God is a jealous God and will not have his place taken by anything else, nor will he be represented by something which does not reflect his true nature.

He alone is God and will not suffer rivals gladly, which leads us to . . .

> *I am the Lord your God who brought you out of the land of Egypt, out of the land of slavery. You shall have no other gods before me.*
> Exodus 20:2–3

We have finally arrived at the beginning!

This Commandment is the one from which all the others flow. It is the starting point; we will not be able to follow the other nine if we do not have this as our axle. It is also the culmination and fulfilment of all the commands. For they do not come in the form of stone tablets dropped from heaven by a God who is distant, a God who is like an angry sergeant major barking commands at us. Instead we are introduced to the God who lays down the basics for living. The world is full of people who do good, who spend their time and money helping others. You might be one of them. As you have read this book you may pride yourself that you are not an adulterer, you have not committed murder, you do not steal and in fact you are really quite honest. You may not be a compulsive liar, you may be satisfied with what you have and not long for bigger and better things; although I'd be very surprised if you could stand with your hand on your heart and say you have never gone against *anything* in the first nine chapters of this book. But what about this one?

In this Commandment we are brought back to basics: what is the place of God in our lives? Not what is the place of the ways of God in our lives, or what do we think of his commands, but what is the place of God? Because the place allotted to him, the position he has in our lives affects everything. Think of it like a wheel, the centre of the wheel is the axle, everything revolves around that. If the axle was off centre, the wheel would not go round smoothly; it would not serve the purpose for which it was made; it would be worse than useless. This is the axle subject: what place we give God in our lives.

So, what does this Commandment begin with? Is there a command for unquestioned devotion or a threat that unless we bow the knee to God we will be exterminated? No, there's not. The most famous set of commands in the history of the world begins with a statement about the one who is giving them:

> I am the Lord your God who brought you out of slavery, out of the land of Egypt.

This could easily be passed over as we move on to the instructions, but if we do not get into focus regarding the one who gives these commands, we shall miss a fundamental truth about this whole topic.

There is a story about an army major who was reading the Old Testament in his country church one Sunday morning. His reading began at Exodus chapter 20, the beginning of the Ten Commandments. He began reading, 'And God spoke all these words . . .' and then added, 'and quite rightly, in my opinion . . .' If we start there we are not starting at the right point. The question is not whether or not we might happen to agree with God. God is not introducing ten suggestions and asking for feedback. This is not a consultative document which is in the process of being put together after a discussion. It really doesn't matter one iota what we personally may make of what follows. What this first statement is all about is introducing to us the God who gives the commands. It is precisely because he is God that we should obey him.

So much of the time we have reduced God to a way-off transcendent being who has absolutely nothing to do with life. The message written by the graffiti artist says it all: 'God is alive—he just doesn't want to get involved.' Other people aren't sure whether he exists, or whether humans have invented the idea of God. As the philosopher Voltaire said, 'If God did not exist he would have to be invented.' Or Nietzsche, who arrogantly asked, 'Is man one of God's blunders or is God one of man's blunders?'

'I am the Lord . . .'

So this passage starts off with a reorientation, a lens through which we must focus to be able to understand everything else. This is a pure and simple declaration of the God who gives these commands. First he is the Lord your God. Now because we are used to the word Lord, the significance can completely pass us by. 'Lord' was the name that God revealed as his own and as we saw in the Third Commandment, names reveal character. The English word 'Lord' is a translation of the Hebrew word 'Yahweh' which means 'I am'. God is the one who exists, the one who is eternal, who always was and always will be. As the great theologian Thomas Aquinas said, 'God is that being beyond which nothing greater can be conceived.'

This whole set of commands begins by God stating something about himself: he is the great 'I am', the ultimate reality. But it is not left there, as if he were some cosmic, impersonal power that demanded allegiance because he has dictatorial tendencies. No, he is the one who is, and he asks the people to look back and remember all that he has done for them. He is the one who has brought them out of slavery in Egypt.

The popular musical *Joseph and His Amazing Technicolor Dreamcoat* has popularised the story of Joseph, the son of Jacob who was sold into slavery in Egypt. He rose to a high position in the country and helped the land through a time of famine. His family eventually joined him in Egypt from the land of Canaan which was suffering greatly under the famine. Because of Joseph all the family were treated well and given their own area to settle in and were left to themselves. Within four generations they became a large and powerful group, but since their origins were in Canaan, a new Pharaoh decided to do some 'ethnic cleansing'. They were all increasingly mistreated and were used as slaves for Pharaoh's ambitious building projects. Life for them was dreadful. As they were a spirited people the Egyptians had to use harsher and harsher methods to keep them under the thumb and so by the time Moses is sent to the people of God, they are at their lowest ebb. They are humiliated, they are slaves, the lowest of the low. Then God reveals himself to Moses at the burning bush. He tells Moses that he has heard the cries of his people in Egypt and has seen their sufferings and is no longer able to stand apart from it. He is going to liberate them and lead them forth from slavery in Egypt to the Promised Land. This is also the point where God reveals his name as 'I am' (Yahweh) to Moses.

Moses goes to Pharaoh to demand the release of God's people and Pharaoh just laughs. God then sends plague after plague on the land until Pharaoh relents and in a moment of desperation gives the word that the people can go, and they flee towards the Red Sea, towards the desert. However, the Egyptians change their minds and follow them. With the vast expanse of the Red Sea in front of them it looks like the people are doomed and will be slaughtered by the Egyptians. But God works a miracle and parts the sea so the people can go through safely to the other side. They are now a free people, they are not slaves, they have left that behind. This is what God has done for them.

This is the God who now gives them basic rules for living. God doesn't start by threatening them, or scaring them; he starts by reminding them of what kind of God he is. He is a God who has acted in history to bring them out of a completely hopeless situation of oppression and slavery and give them liberation and a new start. God reminds them of what he has done for them, of how much he loves them and cares for them and that is why he wants to give them these rules to live by.

The grace of God

And God still does that today. He wants us to do what he says because he loves us and knows what is best for us and not because we are scared stiff of him. Many people ask the question, 'What has God ever done for me?' It is probably quite useful if we just look at some of the things that God has done for us.

It has always been the contention of the Christian church that God's action towards human beings is characterised by grace. That word basically means God's unconditional and never-failing love and care for us. God is a God who goes out of himself to love and care for others. He does not need to. He does not need us in order to be God. We can't contribute anything to him. God is completely able to be, to exist without reference to anything or anyone else. Yet he chooses to bring us into being, to give us life, not because he needs to, but because he wants to because he loves. One answer to the question, 'What has God done for me?' is that he has given you life! And although you perhaps might not feel it at the moment, what a life it is! Have you ever thought what an extraordinary creation you are? The scientist Isaac Newton said, 'In the absence of any other proof, the thumb alone would convince me of God's existence.' God is the one who gives life; you did not bring yourself into existence; you did not give yourself breath. You did not create your own extraordinary complex body. God did.

The world is full of delightful and awe-inspiring sights. Perhaps you have been able to travel the world and see sights which have taken your breath away. The God who made all this is the one who is giving these basic rules for living. They are part of the Maker's instructions. That's why we should follow them— because he knows what is best for us. He is not a remote and distant being but a God who has done much for us.

Again you may say, 'Well, we are not the people who were led from slavery in Egypt. God hasn't done that for us.' You may be looking around at what you have and not feel God has provided a tremendous amount for you.

At this point I want to talk about Jesus. In this command we read that God introduced himself as the living God who had led the people out of slavery to freedom. Now that is what Jesus Christ has done for *all of us*.

You see, every one of us is imprisoned. I'm not talking about our social conditions, or our economic well-being, but the fact that you and I are not free, we are slaves. What to? Well, for a start, we are slaves to ourselves. We are not the people we want to be. I have never met anyone who is truly satisfied with the kind of person that they are. We are disappointed with ourselves, we can't seem to get things right, we mess up the whole time, and in our relationships and our world we hear again and again, 'Things should not be this way.' But we are helpless to do anything. The problem seems too large. And then, as if life was not bad enough, over us hangs the grim certainty of death.

How little we talk about it today, but how real a fear it is. One of the heroes of youth culture, who himself died so young, said, 'What is the thing you respect above all else? That's easy. Death. It's the only thing left to respect. It's the one inevitable, undeniable truth. Everything else can be questioned. But death is truth. In it lies the only nobility for man, and beyond it the only hope.'

Death hangs over us all. People may go to extraordinary lengths to put it off, but they cannot avoid it. Death faces us with the reality that we are not the centre of the world, for we will die and things will continue without us. Death puts it all in perspective.

> If I cast my eyes before me, what an infinite space in which I do not exist! And if I look behind me, what a terrible procession of years in which I did not exist and little space I occupy in this vast abyss of time.
>
> Boussuet, Theologian

Breaking the Commandments of God has the effect of breaking our relationship with God our Creator. That is why for many today God seems so far away. It is important to stress that God did not leave us, but we left him; God did not reject us, but we rejected him; God did not separate himself from us, but we separated ourselves from him.

The way back to God

When there is a breakdown in communication between two parties, we need a mediator. In this case someone who can represent God and represent us. Jesus Christ became the perfect mediator because he was perfect God and perfect man and could therefore represent both God and humankind. Jesus Christ's death on the cross bridged the divide, because by dying he was able to wipe the slate clean. Jesus rose from the dead and therefore authenticates the truth of this.

Jesus then offered his Holy Spirit to any who wanted to be in God's family. When we receive the gift of his Holy Spirit we discover the truth of the words spoken thousands of years ago:

> I will put my law in their minds and write it on their hearts.
>
> (Jeremiah 31:33)

As God was the one who had led his people out of slavery so he is the one who can lead us from slavery today. Throughout the world those who are Christians claim to have found true freedom, freedom from past regrets, a freeing forgiveness, a freedom to be themselves, to live in the relationship with God that they were made for and the freedom to love other people in an unconditional way. And all because of the death and resurrection of Jesus.

In the summer of 1993 I took a team to South Africa to work alongside the church there. We were privileged to meet many South Africans, black and white, who had remained faithful to God and one another during the years of apartheid. Some of the most moving times we had were in the most poor and oppressed areas of that country. We visited churches in the black townships which were full of people who had been put down for the whole of their lives simply because of the colour of their skin; some had been imprisoned, some had been tortured; nearly everyone had lost a member of their family through violence. These were people who from a worldly point of view were not free. Yet they exhibited such deep joy, such real freedom, that the whole team were deeply moved. Of course, social and economic freedom is good and we all should work towards that, but in the face of complete oppression these people had freedom, a freedom which no one could ever take away, which enabled them to face death—a freedom bought by Jesus.

We are not hauled before a judge who has had nothing to do with our lives and told to give him complete, unquestioning allegiance. We are introduced to the God who is alive, who is the ultimate reality, who has not only created us and given us life, but who has worked in the history of the world to win for us and give to us what we were incapable of doing ourselves. It is to this God that we have to listen when he says, 'You shall have no other gods before me.'

This is not something to discuss and debate. There is no question about having him as the number one priority in our life. If God is God then only the most important place for him in our lives will do. The theologian Paul Tillich said, 'Your god is that reality which elicits from you your deepest feelings and your ultimate concern.'

Throughout history men and women have confessed God as their most ultimate concern, not necessarily because they wanted to, but because they have known that if this is true, they must. Even C. S. Lewis described himself as 'the most reluctant convert in the whole of England'. He said he felt as if he had been pursued, that he had no choice in the matter, since he had come to the conclusion that Christianity was true.

There is a similar story of a very strong-minded woman who had been brought up in the Jewish faith, but had become an atheist. She was studying theology in America, but had won a scholarship to Durham University. One afternoon she was walking around the magnificent Cathedral of Durham and came to a figure on the cross. Suddenly she had a very profound realisation that Christianity was true and that meant all she had been promoting and putting forward was false. The words she uttered at this realisation may be left to your imagination!

Now I could have told hundreds of stories of other people who ran headlong as fast as they could into the arms of Jesus, but I wanted to show that people do not simply bow the knee to God because they want to, but because they realise they must.

What about you? Have you been running away from God? Have you been giving God less than first place in your life? Because in this very first command God states that we can have no other gods in his presence.

Those of us within the church are not immune to this. I mentioned earlier the trip I made to South Africa in 1993. We spent a week in Johannesburg, covering some of the most notorious and dangerous areas in the country. Crime was at an all-time high, especially violent crime with guns. With hit-and-run theft and car crime it was becoming a more and more dangerous and frightening place to live. Many South Africans of all races had taken to arming themselves to protect their families, their possessions and their land. The clergy were no exception. But as the peace process continued, it became more and more important that the church set an example as a peace-seeking organisation. This led the Bishop, Peter Lee, to make a decision that no one who was one of his clergy could hold a fire-arm. Most people gave their guns up without too much fuss. But there was a minister who lived in one of the most violent areas of the city. Just two weeks previously a gang had tried to steal his car and he had only been able to save it by threatening them with his gun. He didn't agree with his bishop and refused to give up his gun. In the middle of this dispute, some members of my team went to speak at the church and during the service the minister stood before the packed township church. 'For too long,' he said, 'I have had confidence in a god apart from the true God. I have trusted in my gun. I realise today that I must give up my gun. My security has lain in something other than God.' The congregation were stunned and deeply moved. What they were seeing was full obedience to the first command, 'Have no other gods before me.'

What gods do you have before God? What other gods do you worship? To worship many gods is to have a divided life, drawn this way and that by conflicting desires and conflicting ambitions. I become a whole person when I worship the one true God.

So as we reach the end of our journey through God's Top Ten, we reach the ultimate Number One. What position does God have in our personal life and in our life as a nation? Will you commit yourself to him, to have him as your God, the only one you will live for? For when he says, 'You shall have no other gods before me' the upthrust of it is surely, 'You shall have me.' This is the command to which any breaking of the other nine can be traced. If we put God first we will get everything else in place. There has been much talk about our society being the way it is and wouldn't we do much better if we went back to basics. But the most basic of basics is that we admit that God is Number One, and worship him.

See, I set before you today life and prosperity, death and destruction. For I command you today to love the Lord your God, to walk in his ways, and to keep his commands, decrees and laws; then you will live and increase, and the Lord your God will bless you.

Deuteronomy 30:15